Which came first . . .
   the city or the song?

Music began with time itself;
   the whisper of the wind
      the rhythm of the ocean waves
         the sounds of a gentle rain
Giving life to the melody.

With the poet's words,
   the song was born;
And God gave the song to Nashville.

                              J. Aaron Brown
                              Publisher

"Having been a part of the early years of the Nashville music scene, it is quite a fulfillment to see it become the music center of the United States that it has become. In my opinion, we have the greatest gathering of talent with our songwriters, artists and musicians. And I am very proud to be a part of it all."

— *Wesley Rose*
(Acuff-Rose Publishing)

"Country music songs are direct and unadulterated expressions of the mood and intention of the country fan at any given point in time. It is almost impossible for an ordinary person like a songwriter to predict or play on those moods and intentions. Sometimes we just get lucky."

— *Tom T. Hall*
(Songwriter/Recording Artist)

"Nashville, being a great educational and religious center, was really brought to life with music and the music business."

— *Eddy Arnold*
(Recording Artist)

"Nashville is a product of great songs . . . So is this publication."

— *Jim Black*
(President of National Academy
of Recording Arts and Science –
Nashville Chapter/Vice President
of SESAC, Inc.)

"Songwriters and songs — where it all truly begins!"

— *Tom Collins*
(Producer for Barbara Mandrell &
Ronnie Milsap)

"It all begins with a song — and a songwriter is the individual who makes it all possible. Nashville songs have been recorded in every field of music, and will do nothing but continue to become the music of the world. Hail to the songwriter!"

— *Maggie Cavender*
(Executive Director, Nashville Song-
writers Association, International)

THE SONGS THAT MADE NASHVILLE
MUSIC CITY U.S.A.

Created by:
J. AARON BROWN
Produced by:
DAVID R. LEHMAN
and
ISABEL D. LANDEO

A *PrimeTime* Publication

**HAL LEONARD
PUBLISHING
CORPORATION**

Winona, MN 55987   Milwaukee, WI 53213

FOREWORD

You know the old saying, "Dynamite comes in small packages"? Here is the proof-positive. You now hold in your hands *The Songs That Made Nashville Music City U.S.A.* Yes, these are the songs that launched the careers of numerous recording stars, established some of the largest music publishers in the world, and made several of the major record companies the blockbusters they are today. Also packed between the pages of this convenient, inexpensive, carry-anywhere paperback is a rare collection of interesting photographs and an informative directory of professional music organizations and associations.

When I was first approached about writing the foreword to *The Songs That Made Nashville Music City U.S.A.*, I jumped at the chance because it took but a glance at the list of song titles to be included here to know that this innovative publication would indeed be something different . . . something special!

First and foremost, you'll recognize not one, not two, but *all* of the titles. These are the big ones — the songs that earned Nashville the title **"MUSIC CITY U.S.A."**

Did you know, for instance, that Elvis Presley cut many Nashville songs and recorded at RCA studios on Music Row? You'll find them here: **DON'T BE CRUEL, IT'S NOW OR NEVER, LOVE ME TENDER** and the hit that became the backbone of the huge Nashville publishing empire, Tree International, **HEARTBREAK HOTEL**.

Those Williams boys, Hank and Don, are well-represented too. Hank, whose wailing, emotional vocals made him the king of honky-tonk stylings, still sells records today, 30 years after his death on January 1, 1953. Because of him, **I SAW THE LIGHT, COLD, COLD HEART, JAMBALAYA, YOUR CHEATIN' HEART** and **I'M SO LONESOME I COULD CRY** (later recut by B.J. Thomas) all became standards in the country music field.

The Texas Williams, Don, is noted for tender ballads and gentle, loping tempos. It was his rendition of songwriter Bob McDill's compositions that put both at the top of the heap. **AMANDA** started the ball rolling, then Don went on to stardom with the likes of **GOOD OLE BOYS LIKE ME**.

ROCKY TOP, the highly acclaimed state song of Tennessee, was written by the prolific husband-and-wife writing team of Felice and Boudleaux Bryant. It was the Bryants who put the Everly Brothers on the map with their **BYE BYE, LOVE, ALL I HAVE TO DO IS DREAM**, and **WAKE UP, LITTLE SUSIE**.

Legendary Lefty Frizzell owed his comeback to **LONG BLACK VEIL**, which was purposely written to sound like a traditional folk tune. **RUBY, DON'T TAKE YOUR LOVE TO TOWN** is the song that launched the meteoric rise of Kenny Rogers' solo career.

Who hasn't heard **CRYING MY HEART OUT OVER YOU** lately? The Carl Butler masterpiece was recently revived and made a hit again by Ricky Skaggs.

And long before he was a superstar performer, Willie Nelson was writing standards like Patsy Cline's **CRAZY** and Faron Young's **HELLO WALLS**.

You'll find that guitar virtuoso Merle Travis' blockbuster, **SIXTEEN TONS**, gave the career of Tennessee Ernie Ford the shot in the arm he needed for a comeback.

Rockabilly great Carl Perkins sold a million copies of **BLUE SUEDE SHOES** before Elvis had a hit on the same tune. And it was Perkins' **DADDY SANG BASS** that brought together on stage the Carters and Johnny Cash. Other Cash standards are found here: **I WALK THE LINE, FIVE FEET HIGH AND RISING** and **FOLSOM PRISON BLUES**, which the "man in black" cut twice and made a hit both times.

FLOWERS ON THE WALL made the world sit up and take notice of the wholesome, affable Statler Brothers. Jeannie C. Riley gained fame and fortune with **HARPER VALLEY P.T.A.**, as did David Houston with **ALMOST PERSUADED. LITTLE GREEN APPLES** signaled the comeback of Roger Miller, while **GONE** made Ferlin Husky a household word, and Donna Fargo became **THE HAPPIEST GIRL IN THE WHOLE U.S.A.**

Ray Price and crooner Eddy Arnold helped establish the Nashville Sound, a laid-back feel that was the beginning of adult-oriented country music. Arnold's **ANY TIME** and **MAKE THE WORLD GO AWAY**, and Price's **CRAZY ARMS** are shining examples of the sound that is still prevalent in Nashville studios today.

Along with the traditional standards in *The Songs That Made Nashville Music City U.S.A.*, you'll find that the newer songs by today's artists are also included — songs like Terri Gibbs' **SOMEBODY'S KNOCKIN'** and Anne Murray's **YOU NEEDED ME**. The fabulous boy from Las Vegas, Lee Greenwood, stunned the country with his emotional **IT TURNS ME INSIDE OUT**, while John Anderson took **SWINGIN'**, pronounced it SWANGIN' and had a million-selling country and pop hit.

Furthermore, every song is fully illustrated with diagrams of each easy-to-play guitar chord. Before you know it, you'll be strumming along on such tunes as Ronnie Milsap's **NOBODY LIKES SAD SONGS** or Rick Nelson's **HELLO MARY LOU**.

If I haven't convinced you by now that this will be one of the most "fun" purchases you'll ever make, flip through it . . . check it out . . . I think you'll convince yourself that these are, indeed, *The Songs That Made Nashville Music City U.S.A.!*

Sandy Neese
Music Reporter for
The Nashville Tennessean

COVER STORY

Front Cover: "BROODING IN BLUE," from an original paper sculpture by Reinhard © 1979.

Exclusive Publisher and Distributor: LUNA ART, 1346 WEST WASHINGTON BLVD., VENICE, CALIFORNIA 90291

ABOUT THE ARTIST — Before arriving in the United States in 1961, Reinhard studied graphic design in his native Germany. In the U.S., he continued his education at Art Center School in Los Angeles and The School of Visual Arts in New York. The American Federation of Art selected his fabulous sculpture, "Rehearsal" for the touring exhibit, **200 YEARS OF AMERICAN ILLUSTRATION**, in 1976-77. Reinhard and paper sculpture have become synonymous in today's art world. Many of his works are almost or entirely white paper, relying on reflected light and ambient with all its illusionistic qualities, photographed by the artist to produce the final product. His work has been exhibited in museums and galleries throughout the U.S., Canada, and Europe.

"To the faraway dreamer, she's a flirt and a tease, tempting with the magic of her music. To those of us who walk her streets and know her and love her for all that she is — she is a mother to her children — Nashville."

— *Charles Aaron Wilburn*
  (Songwriter)

CONTENTS

SONG INDEX

NASHVILLE IS 'MUSIC CITY' FOR A REASON

WRITTEN BY
ROBERT K. OERMANN

The story of how Nashville became MUSIC CITY U.S.A. is not an especially long one, for the city has only been a major American recording center for about 25 years. It is a complicated one, however, for there are many reasons why this middle-sized, average, land-locked Southern town became one of the world's entertainment capitals.

The record companies began to send talent scouts into the South in the 1920's. Armed with portable recording equipment, these men set up recording sessions in hotel rooms and invited blues and country musicians in to record. Despite the presence of The Grand Ole Opry, Nashville was not a focal point for these trips. Both Atlanta and Memphis were regional centers for Columbia and Victor (now RCA), not Nashville. Indeed, Nashville didn't host a recording session until the fall of 1928. It was to be nearly 20 years, though, before music recording came to town to stay.

Despite its present renown, The Grand Ole Opry was not the leading country music "barn dance" show, did not have the biggest country music stars, and was not nationally heard weekly until the 1940's. Chicago's WLS National Barn Dance far exceeded it in impact throughout the 1920's and 1930's. The Opry finally went on weekly nationwide radio on NBC in 1943, and around this same time, WLS' talent pool was on the wane.

Throughout the mid- and late-1940's the Opry went on an aggressive talent hunt, attracting such superstars as Bill Monroe, Ernest Tubb, Eddy Arnold, Red Foley, Minnie Pearl, Hank Williams, Roy Acuff, Kitty Wells and Hank Snow to its roster. Some of them joined in the late 1930's, but national radio exposure made them national stars during the war years. The concentration of all this talent in Nashville naturally made the city more attractive as a recording center to the New York record companies.

Three engineers at WSM — George Reynolds, Carl Jenkins and Aaron Shelton — began using the station's old broadcasting studio for recording sessions in the mid-1940's. RCA Victor was on the scene first, once again, and Eddy Arnold's recording for the company in the WSM studio in December, 1944, marked the beginning of the modern Nashville recording industry.

The three engineers' recording operation soon became so successful that they opened their own studio in the old Tulane Hotel downtown (Church St. at Eighth Ave., razed 1956) in 1947. They called their new facility Castle Studios. The first session there was an ad jingle for Shyer's Jewelers sung by Snooky Lanson and featuring Owen Bradley on piano, Harold Bradley on guitar and George Cooper on bass. All three of those musicians were to become pivotal figures in the development on Music Row. Snooky's ad jingle session inaugurated one of the most lucrative and successful parts of the Nashville recording industry, the production of jingles. Today, thousands of these are written and performed in Nashville every year.

The first label to begin holding Nashville sessions on a regular basis was Decca (MCA), which began recording Red Foley and Ernest Tubb at Castle almost immediately after the studio opened. In 1948, the Brown Brothers transcription services opened for business near the corner of Fourth Ave. and Church. This studio was used heavily by RCA until the company shifted its attention to the Methodist Radio and Film Company's studio on McGavock, just behind the area where the gift shops of Hank Williams, Jr. and Conway Twitty now stand near Music Row.

Watchful of the growing recording business, WSM bandleader and pianist Owen Bradley and his guitarist brother Harold decided to get in the ball game. Their first venture, the Bradley Film and Recording Studio, opened at Second Ave. and Lindsley in 1952. They next moved to the building presently occupied by Acme School Supply in Hillsboro Village. Finally, Owen Bradley found a permanent home for his burgeoning business when he built a studio in an old army quonset hut behind a residence at 804 16th Ave. South. It looked like a corrugated metal airplane hangar, but it was nonetheless the first studio built on what became known as Music Row. CBS purchased the quonset hut from Bradley around 1961 and subsequently built a tan brick building around it. It is now CBS office space.

Owen Bradley went on to build Bradley's Barn in Mt. Juliet, Tennessee, and to direct Decca/MCA's country growth, remaining a Nashville music pioneer. Harold Bradley went on to become the dean of MUSIC CITY session guitarists.

RCA executives became even more interested in Nashville in the early 1950's. In the spring of 1957, RCA Studio B opened at 17th Ave. and Hawkins. This event marked the true blossoming of MUSIC CITY recording, for during the next couple of years at this studio, the world-famous "Nashville Sound" was born. The studio is now maintained as an historic site and museum.

By the dawn of the 1960's, the three major country labels — RCA, Columbia and Decca (MCA) — had all set up shop in Nashville. The big companies didn't have the field to themselves, however. As early as 1947, Little Bullet Records had recorded Nashville's first million-seller. The Francis Craig

Orchestra's **NEAR YOU** hit record reportedly led to the establishment of the first record pressing plant in Nashville, and the city is now the second biggest manufacturer of single records in America.

Dot Records, another important early Nashville-founded label, was created by Randy Wood in 1950. It made stars of Pat Boone, the Hilltoppers, Mac Wiseman, Gale Storm and several other pop and country artists. It is significant that both Bullet and Dot (as well as Nashville labels like Hickory and Monument, which followed them) recorded pop music talent. An important factor in Nashville's rise to prominence as a recording center in the 1950's and early 1960's was the status it gained by being the location of pop music million-sellers. Elvis Presley, The Everly Brothers, Brenda Lee, Roy Orbison and Pat Boone drew attention to Music Row from far beyond the country music world.

The construction of the studios, the boom in recording, the gathering of the record labels, and the concentration of Opry talent began to make Nashville a mecca for country musicians by the mid-1950's. Local 257 of The American Federation of Musicians saw its membership swell from 526 in 1950 to 1,638 in 1970; and it has doubled again in the decade since. George Cooper, who played in the historic Castle Studio jingle session, was at the helm of Local 257 from 1937 to 1971; and it was his attitude that allowed the record industry to grow as it did. It was Cooper who changed the union's rules so that country pickers who could not read music could belong. It was Cooper who created the "demo rate" so producers who wanted to experiment without a record contract could do so cheaply. It was Cooper who pioneered the Local AFM's still-standing policy of battling for session-musicians' rights, yet bending rules to make Nashville a cooperative, relaxing place to record. He has received little recognition, but there are many observers who believe the recording industry in MUSIC CITY would never have come to be without George Cooper.

Another big factor in Nashville's rise to prominence as the headquarters for country music was the tireless promotion of MUSIC CITY by the Country Music Association. Founded in 1958, the CMA mounted a publicity and promotional campaign unmatched by any other trade organization. In 1961, there were just 81 full-time country radio stations in America. Twenty years later, due to the CMA's efforts, there were over 2,000. Largely thanks to CMA, Nashville came to be thought of as the country capital.

The CMA, The Opry, the recording studios, the record labels and the stars are the most visible parts of the Nashville music scene. More important than all of these, however, is the music publishing industry in Nashville. As the Nashville Songwriters Association International is fond of pointing out, "It all begins with a song." And in the case of Nashville, it did begin that way.

In 1942, before there were recording sessions in Nashville, before the Opry went on national radio, and before any record label came to town, a Tin Pan Alley songwriter named Fred Rose made an agreement with Grand Ole Opry headliner Roy Acuff and his wife, Mildred, to form a song publishing company for country music in Nashville. The following year, Acuff-Rose Publishing opened for business, the first firm of what became a financial empire in Nashville. Hundreds of song publishing companies have made MUSIC CITY the envy of Los Angeles and New York City, for in recent years artists searching for all kinds of songs have looked to Nashville for material.

Hill and Range, Peer Southern and Tree International followed Acuff-Rose into Nashville in rapid succession in the late 1940's and early 1950's. In the mid-1950's Opry manager Jim Denny and country star Webb Pierce founded Cedarwood Publishing, the company that built the first office building on Music Row.

These companies, and the hundreds which followed them, brought the works of Nashville's brilliant songwriters to fame. Talents like Roger Miller, Willie Nelson, Kris Kristofferson, Bill Anderson, Dolly Parton, Tom T. Hall, Mel Tillis, Don Gibson, Harlan Howard and Rodney Crowell migrated to MUSIC CITY because of the climate created by publishing companies. There is now no better place for a songwriter to be in the English-speaking world than in the midst of the creative cauldron that Nashville has become.

Throughout its growth, Nashville has been known throughout the entertainment world for the goodness and strength of its organizations. Nashville is known as a city where competitors cooperate and pull together for the good of all. It is this spirit of cooperation, the relaxed friendliness, this positive energy that first-time musical guests notice. Perhaps more than any of the other reasons, the intangible hospitality, decency and "quality of life" are what have really built the music industry in Nashville.

It's an industry that brings in some $250 million a year nowadays. It's an industry that has created a huge tourism trade in Tennessee. And it's an industry that has made the capital of the state famous the world over as **MUSIC CITY U.S.A.**

REPRINT COURTESY OF MUSIC CITY NEWS
© Copyright 1983

WHAT IS MUSIC ROW?

Music Row is known throughout the world as "The Street Where Country Music Lives."

While its title may conjure up imagery of a gold-paved thoroughfare lined with music-note-shaped lamp posts, Music Row is actually a very ordinary-looking street. In fact, Music Row is really a pair of rows — two one-way streets, 16th and 17th Avenues South, located just off Interstate 40 in Nashville, Tennessee. From its intersection with Division Street, follow 17th Avenue out of town, cut left across any of several connecting streets onto 16th Avenue, and you will have made the rounds on the famous U-shaped strip that has been the stomping ground for country music songwriters and entertainers for some three decades.

The Music Row area is historic, as it is here where producing pioneer Owen Bradley first located a recording studio on 16th Avenue in 1952, when the terrain was still a residential area. Later Chet Atkins and others were just across the street in the early 1960's, inventing the soon-to-be-called "Nashville Sound" at a facility called Studio B. Slowly but surely, 16th and 17th Avenues became the base of operations for many record labels — RCA, MCA, Monument, Warner Brothers and CBS. You can see the corporate homes of these companies lining the Row today.

As country music grew, many related organizations opened offices in the same locale. These groups include the Country Music Association, The Nashville Songwriters Association International, The Gospel Music Association, the Nashville Musicians' Union Local 257, and publishing arms of such worldwide music licensing agencies as ASCAP, BMI and SESAC. Many entertainers also opened offices on Music Row.

The many facets of country music — recording, publishing, management, promotion, producing and songwriting, to name just a few — all eventually found their way to Music Row. And despite the varied operations of each, they all settled nicely together, side by side along the quiet sidewalks. The one-time square area that is Music Row is an assortment of all kinds of architectural styles, from large, modern office buildings to the original homes converted into offices. The resulting array of old and new gives Music Row a pleasing visual blend, and a suggestion of the area's ties with tradition.

Besides being a business headquarters, Music Row is home for the Country Music Hall of Fame and Museum, along with several other tourist-related shops and exhibits.

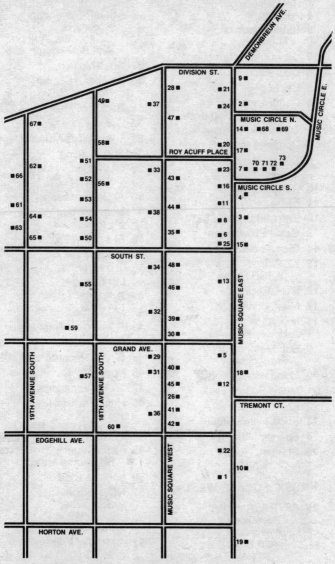

See next two pages for numbered locations.

MUSIC SQUARE EAST

1 ATV Music
2 BMI (Broadcast Music Inc.)
3 Dick Blake International
4 CBS Records
5 CBS Songs
6 Cedarwood Publishing Company
7 Celebration Productions
8 Combine Music Group
9 Country Music Hall Of Fame
10 DebDave Music
11 EMI
12 Emerald Sound Studio
13 Gayle Enterprises
14 Dick James Music
15 KZ Country (WJRB Radio Station)
16 MCA Records
17 Masterfonics Inc.
18 Milk And Honey Records
19 Bob Montgomery Productions
20 Monument Records
21 Music Square Park
22 Pinwheel
23 Pride Music Group
24 Spence Manor Hotel
25 Stargem Records

MUSIC SQUARE WEST

26 AFTRA (American Federation Of Television & Radio Artists)

28 ASCAP (American Society Of Composers, Authors, And Publishers)
29 Ahab Music
30 American Sound Records
31 Buckhorn Music
32 Century II
33 Tom Collins Music
34 FISI Building
35 GMA (Gospel Music Association)
36 Al Gallico Music
37 Hummingbird Productions
38 Al Jolson Music
39 Kings Music City Recorders
40 LSI Studio
41 Don Light Talent
42 MCA Music
43 RCA Studio B (Museum)
44 RCA Records
45 Skylite Records
46 Speer Music
47 Tree International
48 United Artists Tower

18TH AVENUE SOUTH

49 Faded Blue/ Stickhorse Music
50 Fireside Studio
51 NSAI (Nashville Songwriters Association International)
52 OAS/Wild Tracks

19TH AVENUE SOUTH

53 Pete Drake Productions
54 Porter Wagoner
    Enterprises
55 Scott Tutt Music
56 Shook Shack
57 Top Billing

ROY ACUFF PLACE

58 Music Mill Studio

GRAND AVE.

59 Quadrafonic
    Sound Studio

EDGEHILL AVE.

60 Sound Emporium Studio

61 Audio Architects
62 Audio Media
63 J. Aaron Brown &
    Associates, Inc.
64 Dale Morris &
    Associates, Inc.
65 Lorenz Creative
    Services
66 Studio 19
67 Warner Brothers
68 AFM (American
    Federation of
    Musicians)
69 CMA (Country Music
    Assoc.)
70 U.S. Recording Studio
71 Sound Stage
72 Polygram
73 Talbot Bldg.

GREEN GREEN GRASS OF HOME

Words & Music by CURLY PUTMAN

Slowly

The old home town   looks the same __   as I

step   down   from the train,   And there to

meet   me   is   my Ma - ma   and Pa - pa;

And down the road   I   look   and there runs Ma - ry,

hair of gold   and lips like cher -ries.   It's   good   to touch   the

CHORUS

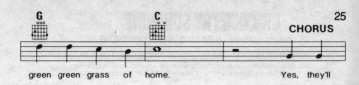

green green grass of home. Yes, they'll

all come to meet me, arms a-reach-ing, smil-ing

sweet-ly. It's good to touch the green green grass of

home. _____ home. _____

2. The old house is still standing tho' the paint is cracked and dry,
   And there's that old oak tree that I used to play on.
   Down the lane I walk with my sweet Mary, hair of gold and lips like cherries;
   It's good to touch the green green grass of home.

3. Then I awake and look around me at the grey walls that surround me,
   And I realize that I was only dreaming,
   For there's a guard and there's a sad old Padre, arm in arm we'll walk at daybreak,
   Again I'll touch the green green grass of home.

CHORUS:
   Yes, they'll all come to see me in the shade of that old oak tree,
   As they lay me 'neath the green green grass of home.

COUNTRY SUNSHINE

Words & Music by BILLY DAVIS & DOTTIE WEST

I was raised on coun-try sun-shine,
raised on coun-try sun-shine, I'm

green __ grass be-neath my feet,
hap-py with the sim-ple things, A

Run-nin' through fields __ of dais-ies and
Sat-ur-day night dance, __ a pic-ture show and the

wad-in' __ through __ the creek.
joy that the blue-bird brings. Now I

love you and it's in-vit-in' to go where
love you, __ please be-lieve me, I would-n't

Bb

life is ___ more ex - cit - in', But I was
want you to ev - er leave me, But I was

C7   1. F

raised on coun - try sun - shine. ___ I was
raised on coun - try

2. F   C7

sun - shine. ___ There's just some - thing a - bout the

F

morn - in', makes each day a joy to

G

see; Night time brings ___ a

peace - ful feel - in' to rest in - side of

me. Yes, I love you, please be -

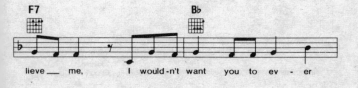

lieve __ me, I would -n't want you to ev - er

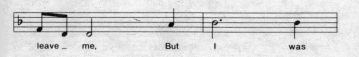

leave __ me, But I was

raised __ on coun - try sun - shine. __

LOVE ME TENDER

Words & Music by ELVIS PRESLEY & VERA MATSON

CRYING MY HEART OUT OVER YOU

**Words & Music by Carl Butler, Marijohn Wilkin,
Louise Certain & Gladys Stacey**

Some - where the mus - ic's play - ing soft and low ____
night I climb the stairs up to my room ____

____ and a stran - ger holds the one that I love
____ it ____ seems I hear you whis - per in the

so. ____ I was blind, I could not see that you
gloom. ____ I miss your pic - ture on the wall and your

meant the world to me But ____ like a fool I
foot - steps in the hall while I'm cry - ing my

stood and watched you go. ____ Now I'm cry - ing my
heart out o - ver you. ____

C7

heart out o - ver you, _____ those blue eyes now, they

F

smile at some - one new. _____ Ev - er

Bb

since you went a - way I die a lit - tle more each

C7

day for I'm cry - ing my heart out o - ver

1. **F**

you. _____ Each

2. **F**

you. _____

KING OF THE ROAD
By ROGER MILLER

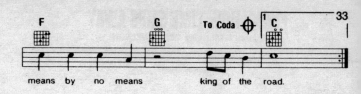

means by no means king of the road.

road I know ev-er-y en-gi-neer on

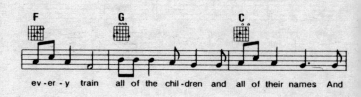

ev-er-y train all of the chil-dren and all of their names And

ev-er-y hand-out in ev-er-y town and

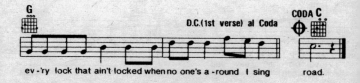

ev-'ry lock that ain't locked when no one's a-round I sing road.

FUNNY HOW TIME SLIPS AWAY

Words & Music by WILLIE NELSON

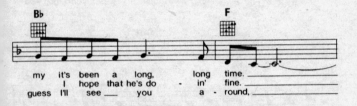

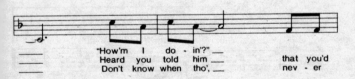

It's been so long now _ and it
Now, that's the same thing__ that you
But re-mem-ber _ what I

F7   Bb

seems that   it was on - ly yes-ter-
told me,   seems like just _ the oth-er
tell you,   that in time _ you're gon-na

G7   C7

day. _ Gee, ain't it fun - ny _ how
day. _ Gee, ain't it fun - ny _ how
pay, _ And it's sur-pris-ing _ how

1,2
F   Bb   F   C7

time   slips a - way. _ How's your
time   slips a - way. _ Got - ta
time   slips a -

3
F   Bb   F

way. _

FOLSOM PRISON BLUES

Words & Music by JOHNNY CASH

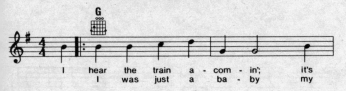

I   hear   the   train   a - com - in';   it's
I   was   just   a   ba - by   my

roll - in'   'round   the   bend,   And
ma - ma   told   me,   "Son, _____

I   ain't   seen   the   sun - shine   since
al - ways   be   a   good   boy;   don't

I   don't   know   when.   I'm
ever   play   with   guns.   But I

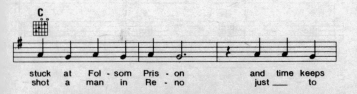

stuck   at   Fol - som   Pris - on   and   time   keeps
shot   a   man   in   Re - no   just ___   to

G

drag - gin' on. _____
watch him die. _____

But that
When I

D7

train keeps roll - in'
hear that whistle blow - in'

on down to San _____ An -
I hang my head _____ and _____

G

tone. _____
cry. _____

When

YOUR CHEATIN' HEART
Words & Music by HANK WILLIAMS

Moderately

Your cheat - in' ___ heart ___ will make you
heart ___ will pine some -

weep ___ You'll cry and ___ cry ___
day ___ And crave the ___ love ___

___ and try to sleep ___ But sleep won't ___
___ you threw a - way ___ The time will ___

come ___ the whole night through ___
come ___ when you'll be blue ___

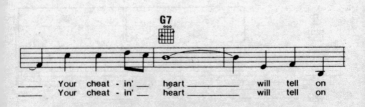

___ Your cheat - in' ___ heart ___ will tell on
___ Your cheat - in' ___ heart ___ will tell on

you _____ When tears come down _____ like fall - in'
you _____ When tears come down _____ like fall - in'

rain _____ You'll toss a - round _____ and call my
rain _____ You'll toss a - round _____ and call my

name _____ You'll walk the _ floor _____ the way I
name _____ You'll walk the _ floor _____ the way I

do _____ Your cheat - in' _ heart _____ will tell on
do _____ Your cheat - in' _ heart _____ will tell on

you. _____ Your cheat - in' _____ you. _____

ROCKY TOP

Words & Music by BOUDLEAUX BRYANT & FELICE BRYANT

Wish that I was on ol' Rock-y Top,
Once two stran-gers climbed ol' Rock-y Top,

down in the Tenn-es-see hills;
lookin' for a moon-shine still;

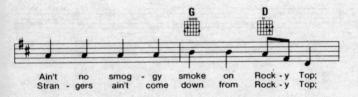

Ain't no smog-gy smoke on Rock-y Top;
Stran-gers ain't come down from Rock-y Top;

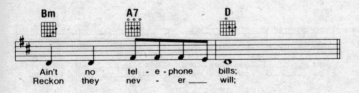

Ain't no tel-e-phone bills;
Reckon they nev-er ___ will;

Once I had a girl on Rock-y Top;
Corn won't grow at all on Rock-y Top;

41

Half bear, oth-er half cat;
Dirt's too rock-y by far;

Wild as a mink, but sweet as so-da pop,
That's why _ all the folks on Rock-y Top

I still dream a-bout that;
get their corn _ from a jar;

Rock-y Top, you'll al - ways be

home sweet home to me;

Good ol' Rock-y Top;

Rock-y Top, Tenn - es - see;

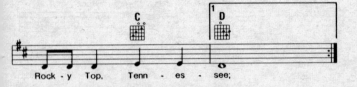

Rock-y Top, Tenn - es - see;

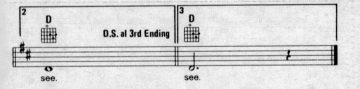

see. see.

D.S. al 3rd Ending

3. I've had years of cramped-up city life
   Trapped like a duck in a pen;
   All I know is it's a pity life
   Can't be simple again. (Chorus)

COLD, COLD HEART
Words & Music by HANK WILLIAMS

Moderately

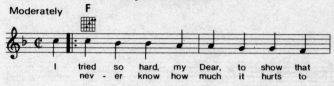

I tried so hard, my Dear, to show that
nev - er know how much it hurts to

You're my ev - 'ry dream   Yet you're a - fraid each
see you sit and cry   You know you need and

thing I do is just some e - vil
want my love yet you're a - fraid to

scheme   A mem - 'ry from your lone - some past keeps
try   Why do you run and hide from life? To

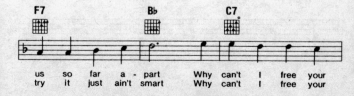

us so far a - part   Why can't I free your
try it just ain't smart   Why can't I free your

44

doubt - ful mind and melt your cold, cold
doubt - ful mind and melt your cold, cold

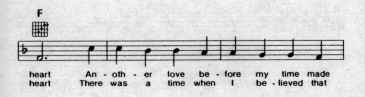

F

heart An - oth - er love be - fore my time made
heart There was a time when I be - lieved that

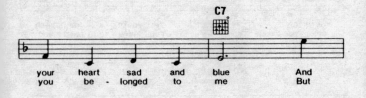

C7

your heart sad and blue And
you be - longed to me But

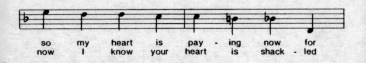

so my heart is pay - ing now for
now I know your heart is shack - led

F

things I did - n't do In
to a mem - o - ry The

an - ger, un - kind words are said that
more I learn to care for you the

F7   **Bb**

make the tear - drops start Why
more we drift a - part Why

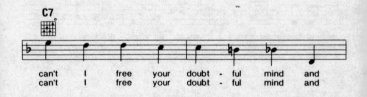

C7

can't I free your doubt - ful mind and
can't I free your doubt - ful mind and

1   **F**

melt your cold, cold heart. You'll

2   **F**

melt your cold, cold heart.

BLUE SUEDE SHOES

By CARL LEE PERKINS

Well, it's one for the mon-ey, two for the show,

three to get read-y, now go, cat, go! But don't you

step on my blue suede shoes. You can

do an-y-thing __ but lay off of my blue suede shoes __

Well, you can knock me down, __ step in my face, __
Burn my house, __ steal __ my car, __

slan-der my name all o-ver the place;— Do an-y-thing that you
drink__ my cider from my old fruit jar;—

want to do,__ but uh-uh, hon-ey, lay off of my shoes __

Don't you step on my blue suede shoes. You can

do an-y-thing__ but lay off of my blue suede

shoes. _____ shoes.

Y'ALL COME BACK SALOON

Words & Music by SHARON VAUGHN

Moderately

She played tam - bou - rine___ with a

sil - ver jin - gle and she must have known the words

___ to at least a mil - lion tunes; ___ But the

one most re - quest - ed by the man she knew as

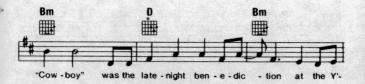

"Cow - boy" was the late - night ben - e - dic - tion at the Y'-

To Verse

A D

all come back sa-loon.___ In a___

Fine %

D G D D

VERSE

voice soft and trem-
night in the shad-

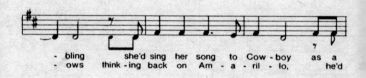

-bling she'd sing her song to Cow-boy as a
-ows think-ing back on Am-a-ril-lo, he'd

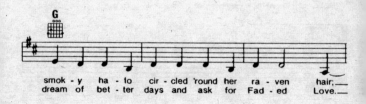

G

smok-y ha-lo cir-cled 'round her ra-ven hair;___
dream of bet-ter days and ask for Fad-ed Love.___

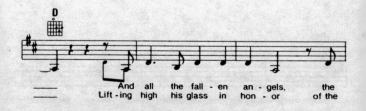

D

And all the fall-en an-gels, the
Lift-ing high his glass in hon-or of the

pin - ball play - in' round - ers   stopped the
la - dy and her song,   he

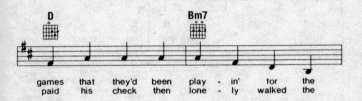

games that they'd been play - in' for the
paid his check then lone - ly walked the

los - ers' eve - ning prayer.
bro - ken cow - boy

home.   Fad - ed Love

and Fad - ed Mem - 'ries, how they____

lin ger in a

mind; _____ Miles and years _

_ played the cow - boy like an

old mel - o - dy, out of tune _

D.S. (to 2nd ending)

and out of time. _____ Ev - 'ry

SIXTEEN TONS

Words & Music by MERLE TRAVIS

Moderately

VERSE

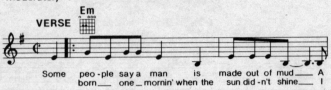

Some peo-ple say a man is made out of mud___ A
born___ one___ mornin' when the sun did-n't shine___ I

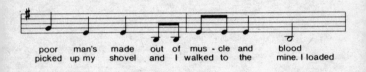

poor man's made out of mus-cle and blood
picked up my shovel and I walked to the mine. I loaded

Mus-cle and blood and skin and bones___ A
six-teen tons of number nine coal And the

mind that's___ weak and a back that's strong, You load
straw-boss___ said "Well-a bless my soul." You load

CHORUS

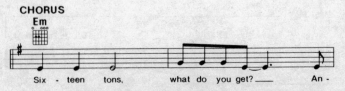

Six-teen tons, what do you get?___ An-

oth-er day old-er and deep-er in debt.___ Saint

Am

Pe-ter, don't you call me 'cause I can't go ___ I

Em

owe ___ my soul to the com-pa-ny store.___

1.

___ I was

2.

SOMEDAY MY DAY WILL COME

Words & Music by EARL MONTGOMERY, CHRISTOPHER C. RYDER & V.L. HAYWOOD

Some-day my day will come, _____

and I won't need a thing at all.

I can stand proud and tall,

and say just what I feel. _____

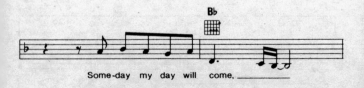

Some-day my day will come, _____

when dreams be-come re - al - i - ty,

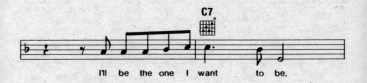

I'll be the one I want to be,

Some-day my day will come.

It's a tir - ing path we ___

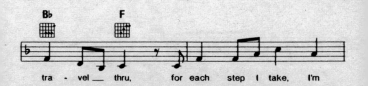

tra - vel ___ thru, for each step I take, I'm

set back two. We all have roles in

life __ to __ play, and I'll play a great one some-

day. Some-day my day will come ____

I'll watch my ship as it comes __ in

I'll touch the pret-ty rain - bow's end, ____

and my cup will o - ver - flow. _____

Some-day my day will come, _____

I'll hold true love right in ___ my hand,

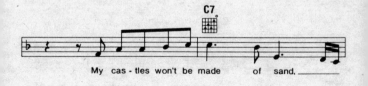

My cas - tles won't be made of sand. _____

Some-day my day will come. _____

THANK GOD AND GREYHOUND

Words & Music by LARRY KINGSTON & ED NIX

Slow

VERSE

I've made a small for - tune and you've
Now you come to me with a

squan - dered it all. You shamed me 'till
sim - ple good-bye. You tell me you're

I feel ___ a - bout one inch tall.
leav - ing but you don't tell me why. ___

___ But ___ I thought I loved you and I
___ Now we're here at the sta - tion and

hoped you would change. So I grit - ted my
you're get - ting on. And all I can

teeth and I did - n't com -

plain. _____

think of is thank God and Grey - hound you're

gone. _____ CHORUS Thank God and

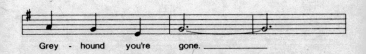

Grey - hound you're gone. _____

I did - n't know how much long - er

I could go on. _____

Watch - ing you take the re - spect out of

me. Watch - ing you make a to - tal

wreck out of me. That

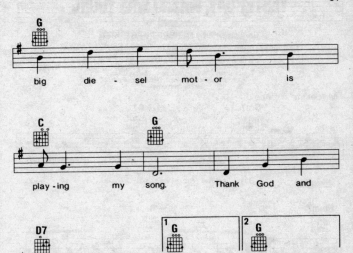

big die - sel mot - or is

play - ing my song. Thank God and

Grey - hound you're gone. gone.

Chorus 2

Oh, thank God and Greyhound you're gone
The load on my mind got lighter when you got on
That shiny old bus is a beautiful sight
With the black smoke rolling up around the taillights.
It may sound kinda cruel, but I've been silent too long
Thank God and Greyhound you're gone.

YESTERDAY, WHEN I WAS YOUNG
(Hier Encore)

English lyric by HERBERT KRETZMER
Original French text and Music by CHARLES AZNAVOUR

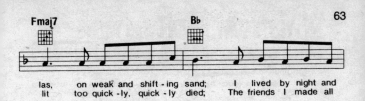

las,   on weak and shift-ing sand;   I lived by night and
lit   too quick-ly, quick-ly died;   The friends I made all

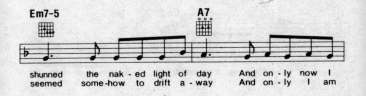

shunned   the nak-ed light of day   And on-ly now I
seemed   some-how to drift a-way   And on-ly I am

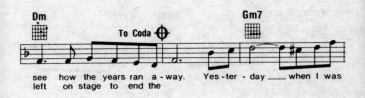

see how the years ran a-way.   Yes-ter-day ___ when I was
left on stage to end the

young,   So man-y drink-ing songs   were wait-ing to be

sung,   So man-y way-ward plea-sures lay in store for

me   And so much pain my daz - zled eyes re-fused to

see,   I ran so fast that time   and youth at last ran

out,   I nev - er stopped to think   what life was all a -

bout   And ev - 'ry con - ver - sa - tion   I can now re -

call   con-cerned it - self with me,   and noth - ing else at

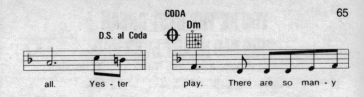

all. Yes - ter

CODA

play. There are so man - y

songs in me that won't be sung, I feel the bit - ter

taste of tears up - on my tongue, The time has come for

me _____ to pay for yes - ter - day when

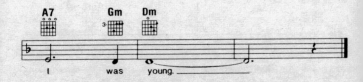

I was young. _____

YOU'RE THE BEST BREAK
THIS OLD HEART EVER HAD

Words & Music by WAYLAND HOLYFIELD & RANDY HATCH

With Movement

Oh, there were oth - ers,

some were friends, ___ some were mere - ly lov - ers.

But they all ___ helped me dis -cov-

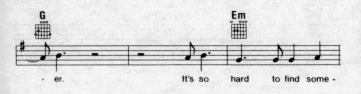

- er. It's so hard to find some -

one who'll be true. ___

I said, "No   way
round   me

would   I   fall   a - gain,   oh, no,
my   world   was crumb - ling   down   all   a -

no   way."
round   me.   There's

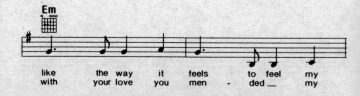

just   too   man - y   heart -aches   And   I   don't
Oh,   but   then   you   found   me   and

like   the   way   it   feels   to   feel   my
with   your love   you   men - ded __   my

68

D   **Am**

heart   break   Then   there   was
life.

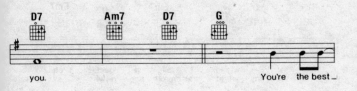

D7   **Am7**   **D7**   **G**

you.   You're the best __

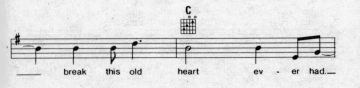

                   C

__ break this old   heart   ev - er had. __

Cmaj7   **Am**   **D**

__   You're all the good __ luck that I'll

G   **Gmaj7**

ev - er need __   to have. __

G7

Nev - er thought I'd ev - er

C   **Em7**   **Am**   **Em7**

love a - gain like that. You're the best break

Am7   **D7**   **Am7**   **D7**   **D11**

this old heart __ ev - er

1
G   **C**

had.

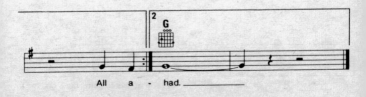

2
G

All a - had. ____

A THING CALLED LOVE

Words & Music by JERRY REED HUBBARD

Medium Country

Six foot six he stood on the ground weighed two___

hun-dred and thir-ty five pounds. But I saw that

gi-ant of a man brought down to his knees by love.

He was the kind of man that would gam-ble on

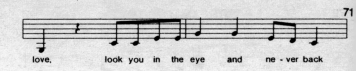

love, look you in the eye and ne - ver back

Dm

up. But I saw him cry - ing like a lit - tle whipped

G7 **C** **CHORUS**

pup be -cause of __ love. Can't see it with your

F

eyes, hold it in your hand, But like the

Em **Am**

wind it co -vers our land, strong e -nough to

rule   the heart of   a - ny   man __   this   thing __ called __

love.   It can lift you up   it can let you

down,   take your   world   turn it all a -

round.   E - ver since   time   no - thing's e - ver been

found   strong - er   than __ love.

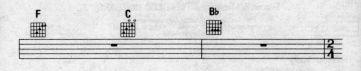

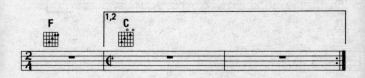

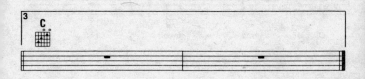

Verse 2. Most men are like me they struggle in doubt
They trouble their mind day in and day out
Too busy with living to worry about a word called love
(Chorus)

3. But when I see a mother's tenderness
As she holds her young close to her breast
Then I thank God this world's been blessed with a word
called love.
(Chorus)

U.S. MALE

Words & Music by JERRY REED HUBBARD

Moderately

CHORUS

So you bet - ter not mess with the

U. S. male my friend.

If the U. S. male gets

mad He's gon - na do you in.

If you know what's good for your-

self   son, you'll go   find   you   some -bo - dy

else,   Son   don't   tam -per with the pro -per -ty

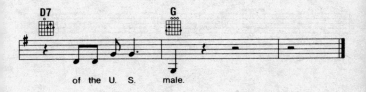

of the U. S.   male.

RECITATION

1. Now I'm a U.S. male cause I was born in a south Georgia town on a
Sunday morn
Now Georgia just happens to occupy a place in the south-eastern portion
of these United States
Now that's a fact buddy and you know it well
So I just call myself the U.S. Male M.A.L.E. son that's me
Now I said all that and I'll say all this
I been a-watching the way you been a-watching my miss
For the past three weeks you been hot on her trail
You're kinda upsetting the U.S. Male
Now you touch her once with your greasy hand
I'm gonna stretch your neck like a long rubber band
Cause she's wearing a ring that I bought on sale
So that makes her property of this U.S. Male (CHORUS)

2. Through the rain and the heat and the sleep and the snow
The U.S. Male is on his toes
So quit watching my woman cause that ain't wise
You ain't pulling no wool over this boy's eyes
Now I catch you around my woman champ
I'm gonna leave your head like the shape of a stamp
Kinda flattened out so you'd do well
To quit playing games with the U.S. Male (CHORUS)

WHEN TWO WORLDS COLLIDE

By ROGER MILLER & BILL ANDERSON

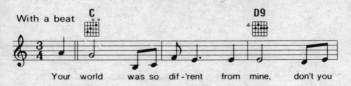

Your world was so dif-'rent from mine, don't you

see and we could-n't be close, though we

tried, _____ we both reached for

heav-ens, but ours weren't the same that's what

hap-pens When two worlds col - lide. _____

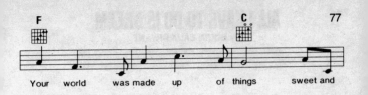

Your world was made up of things sweet and

good. My world could nev - er fit

in, Wish it could. Two hearts lie in

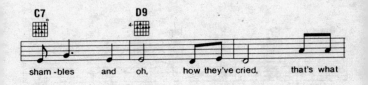

sham -bles and oh, how they've cried, that's what

hap -pens When two worlds col - lide. _____

ALL I HAVE TO DO IS DREAM

By BOUDLEAUX BRYANT

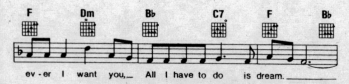

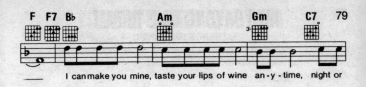

I can make you mine, taste your lips of wine an-y-time, night or

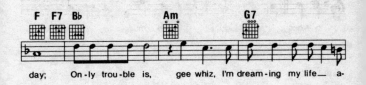

day; On-ly trou-ble is, gee whiz, I'm dream-ing my life a-

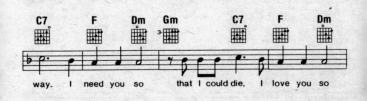

way. I need you so that I could die, I love you so

and that is why When-ev-er I want you, All I have to do is

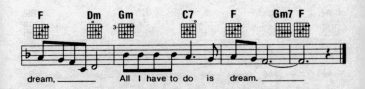

dream, All I have to do is dream.

ARE YOU LONESOME TONIGHT?

Words & Music by ROY TURK AND LOU HANDMAN

Moderate Waltz Tempo

Are you lone-some to-night, Do you miss me to-

night, Are you sor-ry we drift-ed a-

part? _____ Does your mem-o-ry

stray to a bright sum-mer day, when I

kissed you and called you sweet-heart? _____ Do the

chairs   in   your   par - lor   seem emp - ty   and

bare?   Do you gaze   at   your door - step   and pic - ture   me

there?   Is your heart   filled   with pain,   Shall I come back a-

gain?   Tell me, dear,   Are   you   lone - some   to -

night?   Are you   night? _____

ANY TIME

Words & Music by HERBERT HAPPY LAWSON

Moderately

An-y time _____ you're feel-ing lone - ly, _____

_____ An - y time _____ you're feel-ing blue, _____

_____ An - y time _____ you feel down-

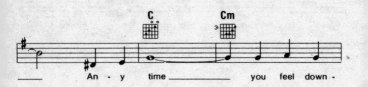

heart - ed. _____ That will prove your

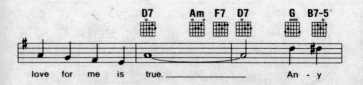

love for me is true. _____ An - y

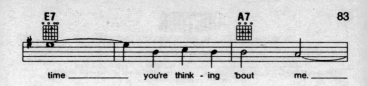

time _____ you're think - ing 'bout me. _____

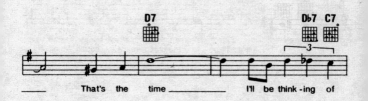

_____ That's the time _____ I'll be think - ing of

you, _____ So an - y time you

say you want me back a - gain, That's the

time I'll come back home to you. _____

DETOUR

Words & Music by PAUL WESTMORELAND

Moderately

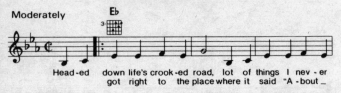

Head-ed   down life's crook-ed road,   lot of things I nev-er
got right   to   the place where it   said "A-bout _

knowed,   And 'cause of   me   not know-in'   I   now
Face,"   I   thought that   all   my   wor-ries   were be-

pine. _____   Troub-le got   in   the trail   spent the
hind. _____   But the far-ther I   go   the more

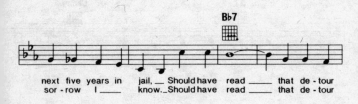

next five years in   jail, _ Should have   read _____ that de-tour
sor-row   I _____   know. _ Should have   read _____ that de-tour

sign. _____
sign. _____   }   De-   tour, _____   There's a

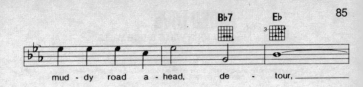

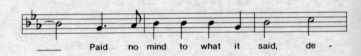

mud - dy road a - head, de - tour, _____

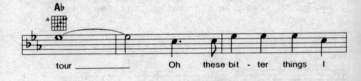

_____ Paid no mind to what it said, de -

tour _____ Oh these bit - ter things I

find, should have read _____ that de - tour

sign. _____ When I | sign. _____

FADED LOVE

Words & Music by JOHN WILLS & BOB WILLS

Moderately

As I look at the let - ters that you wrote to
think of the past and all the pleas - ures we

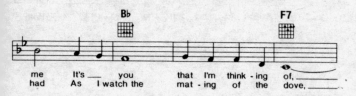

me It's ___ you that I'm think - ing of, ___
had As I watch the mat - ing of the dove, ___

___ As I read the lines ___ that to
___ It was in the spring ___ time that

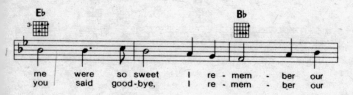

me were so sweet I re - mem - ber our
you said good-bye, I re - mem - ber our

CHORUS

fad - ed love. ___
fad - ed love. ___   I miss you

darling more and more ev - 'ry day As

heav - en would miss the stars a - bove.____ With

ev - 'ry heart - beat I still think of

you And re - mem - ber our fad - ed

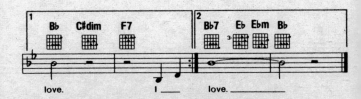

love.   I ___   love. _____

A BOY NAMED SUE

Words & Music by SHEL SILVERSTEIN

Moderately Bright

Verse I
(Recitative)

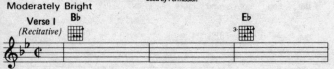

Well, my daddy left home when I was three, and he didn't leave

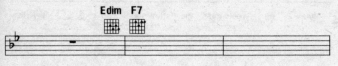

much to ma and me, Just this old guitar and an empty

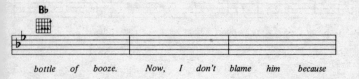

bottle of booze. Now, I don't blame him because

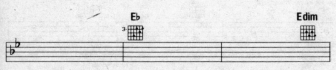

he run and hid, but the meanest thing that he ever did was

before he left, he went and named me Sue.

Well, he must have thought it was

quite a joke, And it got lots of laughs from a lots of folks,

It seems I had to fight my whole life through.

Some gal would giggle and I'd get red, And

some guy would laugh and I'd bust his head, I tell you, life ain't

easy for A Boy Named Sue.

Repeat for additional verses
(3-4, 5-6, 7-8)

Last time (9-10)

Well,

3. (Well,) I grew up quick and I grew up mean,
   My fist got hard and my wits got keen.
   Roamed from town to town to hide my shame,
     but I made a vow to the moon and stars,
   I'd search the honky tonks and bars and kill that man
     that give me that awful name.

4. But it was Gatlinburg in mid July
     and I had just hit town and my throat was dry.
   I'd thought I'd stop and have myself a brew.
   At an old saloon on a street of mud
   And at a table dealing stud
     sat the dirty, mangy dog that named me Sue.

5. Well I knew that snake was my own sweet dad
     from a worn-out picture that my mother had.
   And I know that scar on his cheek and his evil eye.
   He was big and bent and gray and old
   And I looked at him and my blood ran cold,
     and I said "My name is Sue. How do you do.

   Now you're gonna die. "Yeah, that's what I told him.

6. Well I hit him right between the eyes and he went down,
     but to my surprise he come up with a knife
   And cut off a piece of my ear. But I busted a chair right across his teeth.
   And we crashed through
   The wall and into the street kicking and a-gouging
     in the mud and the blood and the beer.

7. I tell you I've fought tougher men
     but I really can't remember when.
   He kicked like a mule and he bit like a crocodile.
   I heard him laughin' and then I heard him cussin',
   He went for his gun and I pulled mine first.
   He stood there looking at me and I saw him smile,

8. And he said, "Son, this world is rough
     and if a man's gonna make it, he's gotta be tough
   And I know I wouldn't be there to help you along.
   So I give you that name and I said 'Goodbye,'
   I knew you'd have to get tough or die.
   And it's that name that helped to make you strong.

9. Yeah, he said now you have just fought one helluve fight,
     and I know you hate me and you've
   Got the right to kill me now and I wouldn't
     blame you if you do. But you ought to thank me
   Before I die for the gravel in your guts
     and the spit in your eye because I'm the — — — —
   That named you Sue."

   Yeah, what could I do? What could I do?

10. I got all choked up and I threw down my gun.
    Called him a pa and he called me a son,
    And I come away with a different point of view.
    And I think about him now and then.
    Every time I tried, every time I win and if I
    ever have a son I think I am gonna name him
    Bill or George - - anything but Sue.

COUNTRY BUMPKIN

Words & Music by DON WAYNE

His   big round ears were stick-ing out be - neath the straw hat
walked in - to the bar and placed his   lank - y frame up -

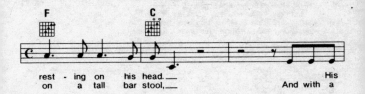

rest - ing on   his head. ___
on   a tall   bar stool, ___   And with a   His

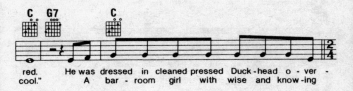

hon - est face was weath-ered and his nose was a shin-ey sun - burned
long, soft south-ern drawl, said, "I'll just have a glass of an - y - thing that's

red.   He was dressed in cleaned pressed Duck - head o - ver -
cool."   A   bar - room girl   with wise and know - ing

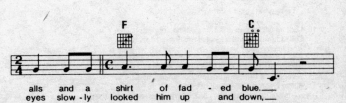

alls   and a   shirt   of fad - ed blue. ___
eyes slow - ly looked him up   and down, ___

G7

You could look at him and al - most smell the
And she thought, "I won - der how on earth that

1 **C**

barn - yard on his scuffed - up Bro - gan shoes.   He
coun - try bump - kin found his way to

2,3,4 C

Chorus   **F**

town."   And she said, "Hel - lo, coun - try bump - kin,

G7   **C**

How's the frost out on the pump - kins? _____

F

I've seen some sights, but, boy, you're some - thing _____

G7   C   1,2   3

Where'd you come from, coun-try bump-kin?"

3. Just a short year later in a sweat-drenched bed of
      joy and tears and death-like pain,
   Into this wondrous world of many wonders,
      one more wonder came.
   That same woman's face was wrapped up
      in a raptured look of love and tenderness,
   As she marvelled at the soft and warm
      and cuddly boy-child suckin' at her breast.
CHORUS:
   And she Said, "Hello, Country bumpkin,
      fresh as frost out on the pumpkins;
   I've seen some sights, but babe, you're somethin'!
   Mama loves her Country bumpkin."

4. Forty years of hard work later,
      in a simple quiet and peaceful country place,
   The heavy hand of time had not erased
      the raptured wonder from the woman's face.
   She was lying on her death bed
      knowing fully well her race was nearly run,
   But she softly smiled and looked up
      at the sad eyes of her husband and her son.
CHORUS:
   And she said, "So long, Country bumpkins,
      the frost is gone now from the pumpkins.
   I've seen some sights, and life's been somethin'.
   See you later, Country bumpkins."

CRAZY ARMS

Words & Music by RALPH MOONEY & CHARLES SEALS

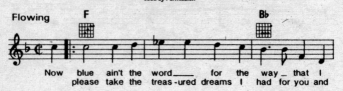

Now blue ain't the word____ for the way __ that I
please take the treas-ured dreams I had for you and

feel, and the storms brew-ing in this heart of
me and ___ take all the love I thought was

mine. _____ This ain't no cra-zy dream, I
mine. _____ Some-day my cra-zy arms may

know ____ that it's real, you're some-one els- e's
hold some-bod-y new, but now ___ I'm so

love now; You're not mine. _____ }
lone-ly all the time.

Cra - zy arms that reach to hold some-bod - y

new, for my yearn - ing heart keeps say - in' you're not

mine. ___ My trou - bled mind knows soon, to an -

oth - er you'll be wed, and that's why I'm

lone - ly all the time. ___ So ___

DON'T BE CRUEL
(TO A HEART THAT'S TRUE)
By OTIS BLACKWELL & ELVIS PRESLEY

Medium Bright

You know I can be found_ sit-ting home all a-
Baby, if I made you mad for some-thing I might have

lone   If you can't come a - round,   At
said   Please let's forget the past   The

least, please tel - e - phone.   Don't be cruel _____
future looks bright a - head.   Don't be cruel _____

_____ to a heart that's true. _____
_____ to a heart that's

true. _____   I don't want no oth - er love,

Ba - by, it's just you I'm think - ing of. _____

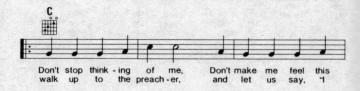

Don't stop think - ing of me, Don't make me feel this
walk up to the preach - er, and let us say, "I

way, Come on o - ver here and love me, You
do." Then you'll ___ know you have me, And I'll

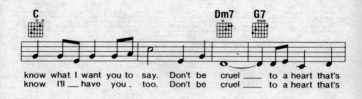

know what I want you to say. Don't be cruel ___ to a heart that's
know I'll ___ have you ___ too. Don't be cruel ___ to a heart that's

true. _____ Why should we be a - part? I
true. _____ I don't want no oth - er love,

HAVE I TOLD YOU LATELY THAT I LOVE YOU

Words & Music by SCOTT WISEMAN

Have I told you late - ly that I
told you late - ly how I
told you late - ly when I'm

love you? _____ Could I tell you
miss you _____ when the stars are
sleep - ing _____ ev - 'ry dream I

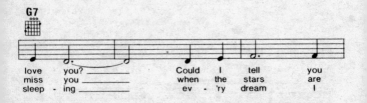

once a - gain some - how? _____ Have I
shin - ing in the sky? _____ Have I
dream is you some - how? _____ Have I

told with all my heart and
told you why the nights and are
told you who I'd like to

real - ly love you, ba - by, cross my heart. _____ Let's
Ba - by, it's just you I'm think -ing

of. _____ Don't be cruel _____ to a heart that's

true. _____ Don't be cruel _____ to a heart that's

true. _____ I don't want no oth - er love

Ba - by, it's just you I'm think -ing of. _____

| C | Cdim | C | F | C | C#dim |

soul how I a - dore you? Well,
long when you're not with me? Well,
share my love for - ev - er? Well,

| G7 | | | C | Fm | F |

dar - ling, I'm tell - ing you now. ____
dar - ling, I'm tell - ing you now. ____
dar - ling, I'm tell - ing you now. ____

| C | C7+5 | F |

____ } This heart would break in two if you re -

| C | C#dim | G7 |

fuse me. ____ I'm no good with -

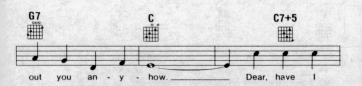

| G7 | C | C7+5 |

out you an - y - how. ____ Dear, have I

101

told you late - ly that I

love you? _____ Well,

dar - ling, I'm tell - ing you

now. Have I
Have I

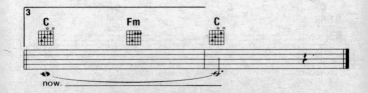
now. _____

THE HAPPIEST GIRL IN THE WHOLE U.S.A.

Words & Music by DONNA FARGO

love wak-in' up next to me as much as I

love wak-in' up next to you.___ You make the

you be care - ful, got -ta go. I love you ___

Have a beau -ti - ful day___ And kiss the hap - pi - est

girl ____ in the whole ___ U. S. A.

Skip - a - dee - doo - dah __ Thank you Lord, for

mak - ing him for me __ And thank you for let - ting life

turn out the way that I al - ways thought it could

be. _____ There once was a time when I

could not im - ag - ine __ how it would feel __ to

say   I'm the hap - pi - est girl____   in the

whole _____ U. S. A, _____   Now

shine on me sun - shine walk with me, world, it's a

skip - a dee - doo - dah day,   And I'm the hap - pi - est

girl __   in the whole ____ U. S. A. _____

GONE

Words & Music by SMOKEY ROGERS

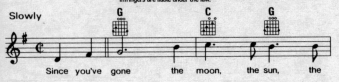

Slowly

Since you've gone   the moon,   the sun,   the

stars in the sky   know   the rea - son   why__ I   cry.

Love __ di - vine   once was mine,   now you've

gone. _____   Since you've gone   my

heart, my lips, my tear - dimmed eyes, a lone - ly soul with -

in __ me cries, I act - ed smart, broke __ your heart;

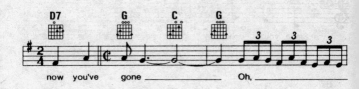

now you've gone _____ Oh, _____

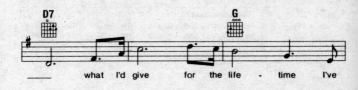

____ what I'd give for the life - time I've

wast - ed the love that I've tast - ed. I ___ was

wrong, now you've gone. _____

FIVE FEET HIGH AND RISING

Words & Music by JOHNNY CASH

With a beat

How high is the wa - ter, Ma - ma? Two feet high and
How high is the wa - ter, Ma - ma? Three feet high and

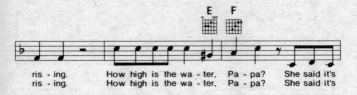

ris - ing. How high is the wa - ter, Pa - pa? She said it's
ris - ing. How high is the wa - ter, Pa - pa? She said it's

two feet high and ris - ing. But we can
three feet high and ris - ing. Well, the

make it to the road in a home - made boat, 'cause that's the
hives are _ gone; _ I lost my bees;

on - ly thing we _ got _ left that - 'll float. It's
chick - ens are sleep - in' in the wil - low _ trees.

al - read-y o - ver all the wheat and oats.
Cows in ___ wa - ter up ___ past their knees.

Two feet high and ris - ing.
Three feet high and ris - ing.

Guitar Tacet

ris - ing, well, it's five feet high and ris - ing.

3. How high is the water, Mama?
   Four feet high and rising.
   How high is the water, Papa?
   She said it's four feet high and rising.
   Hey, come look through the window pane;
   The bus is comin' gonna take us to the train.
   Looks like we'll be blessed with a little more rain. Four feet high and rising.

4. How high is the water, Mama?
   Five feet high and rising.
   How high is the water, Papa?
   She said it's five feet high and rising.
   Well, the rails are washed out north of town;
   We gotta head for higher ground.
   We can't come back till the water goes down.
   Five feet high and rising;
   Well, it's five feet high and rising.

DON'T TAKE YOUR GUNS TO TOWN

Words & Music by Johnny Cash

Moderately

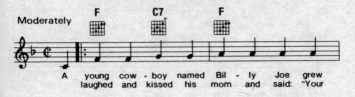

A young cow-boy named Bil-ly Joe grew
laughed and kissed his mom and said: "Your

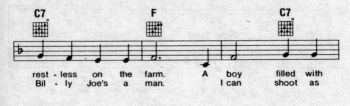

rest-less on the farm. A boy filled with
Bil-ly Joe's a man. I can shoot as

wan-der-lust, who real-ly meant no harm. He
quick and straight as an-y-bod-y can. But I

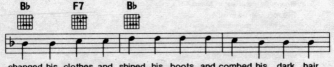

changed his clothes and shined his boots and combed his dark hair
would-n't shoot with-out a cause; I'd gun no-bod-y

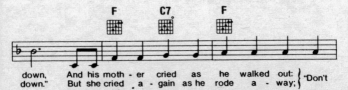

down, And his moth-er cried as he walked out: { "Don't
down." But she cried a-gain as he rode a-way; {

take your guns to town, son; Leave your guns at

home, Bill; don't take your guns to

town." He town." _____

3. He sang a song as on he rode, his guns hung at his hips.
   He rode into a cattle town, a smile upon his lips.
   He stopped and walked into a bar and laid his money down,
   But his mother's words echoed again: "Don't Take Your Guns To Town, son;
   Leave your guns at home, Bill; Don't Take Your Guns To Town."

4. He drank his first strong liquor then to calm his shaking hand,
   And tried to tell himself at last he had become a man.
   A dusty cowpoke at his side began to laugh him down.
   And he heard again his mother's words: "Don't Take Your Guns To Town, son;
   Leave your guns at home, Bill; Don't Take Your Guns To Town."

5. Bill was raged and Billy Joe reached for his gun to draw.
   But the stranger drew his gun and fired before he even saw.
   As Billy Joe fell to the floor the crowd gathered 'round
   And wondered at his final words: "Don't Take Your Guns To Town, son;
   Leave your guns at home, Bill, Don't Take Your Guns To Town."

A BROKEN HEARTED ME

Words & Music by RANDY GOODRUM

Slowly, with feeling

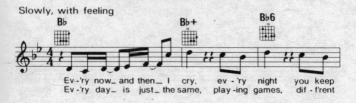

Ev--'ry now_ and then_ I cry,   ev-'ry night   you keep
Ev'ry day_ is just_ the same,   play-ing games,   dif-f'rent

stay-in' on my mind.___   All   my   friends say I'll sur-vive,_
lov-ers, dif-f'rent names___   They keep say-in' I'll sur-vive._

it just takes time,)
it just takes time,}   but I don't think time is gon-na heal_

___ this bro-ken heart.___   No, I don't see how_ it can_ if it's

bro-ken all_ a-part.___   A mil-lion mir-a-cles_ could nev-

- er stop_ the pain, _ or put all the piec - es to-

geth - er a - gain. _ No, I don't think time is gon - na heal_

_ this bro - ken heart, _ No, I don't see how_ it can_ while

we are still_ a -part. _ And when you hear_ this song_ I

hope that you_ will see_ that time won't heal_ a bro -ken -heart -ed

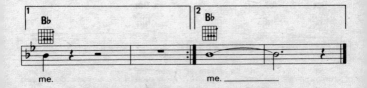

me.   me. _____

DREAM ON LITTLE DREAMER

Words & Music by FRED B. BURCH & JAN CRUTCHFIELD

Relaxed tempo

Dream on lit-tle dream-er dream on

Dream on lit-tle dream-er dream

on ____ I get a heart full of

but-ter-flies look-ing in-to your dream-y eyes dream

on lit-tle dream-er dream on dream

on   lit - tle dream -er dream on   Dream

F   **A7**

on   lit - tle dream -er dream   on _____

Dm   **Gm**

Dream -a -bout   a love so true   dream a -bout   how

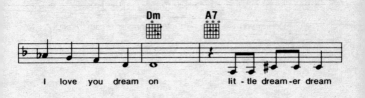

Dm   **A7**

I love you dream on   lit - tle dream -er dream

Dm   **Gm**

on   You know I love   you   I

Dm

love you and I need you so   bad _____

116

Each night I re - al - ize when you close your

dream - y eyes you dream on lit - tle dream - er dream on

Dream on lit - tle dream - er dream on ____

Dream a - bout a love so fine sweet as ap - ple

ber - ry wine dream on lit - tle dream - er dream on.

I AIN'T NEVER

Words & Music by MEL TILLIS & WEBB PIERCE

Moderately, with a strong beat

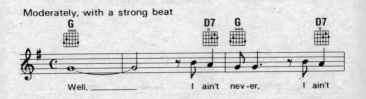

Well, _____ I ain't nev-er, I ain't

nev-er, seen no-bod-y like

you, no, no, no, Nev-er have I

ev-er seen no-bod-y like you.

You call me up _____ an' say to
tell me sweet things that

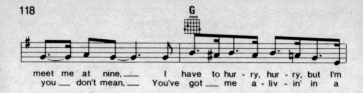

meet me at nine,___ I have to hur - ry, hur - ry, but I'm
you ___ don't mean,___ You've got ___ me a - liv - in' in a

there on time,___ I walk - a right up ___ an'
haunt - ed dream,___ You make me do things___ I

knock on your door,___ The land - lord says, "She ain't a
don't want to do, ___ My friends - a say, "Webb - a, what's___

here no ___ more"} I ain't nev - er, oh,
wrong with you."}

dar - ling, seen no - bod - y like

you, boo, hoo, but I love you, yeah, I

love you, I love you just the same.

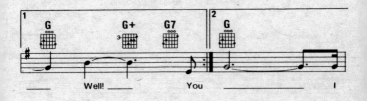

_____ Well! _____ You _____ I

love you just the same, _____ I

love you just the same. _____

I FALL TO PIECES

Words & Music by HANK COCHRAN & HARLAN HOWARD

act like we've nev - er kissed; _____ you
find some - one else to love, _____ you some -

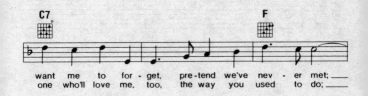

want me to for - get, pre - tend we've nev - er met; _____
one who'll love me, too, the way you used to do; _____

_____ And I've tried _____ and I've tried, but I
_____ But each time _____ I go out with _____

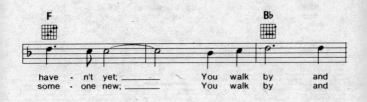

have - n't yet; _____ You walk by and
some - one new; _____ You walk by and

I fall to piec - es. _____
I fall to piec - es. _____

IF DRINKIN' DON'T KILL ME, HER MEMORY WILL

Words & Music by RICK BERESFORD & HARLAN SANDERS

The bars are all closed, ___ it's
old bones they move slow, but so

four in the morn — ing, Must-'ve shut 'em all
sure of their foot - steps, As I trip on the

down ___ by the shape that I'm
floor ___ and light - ly touch

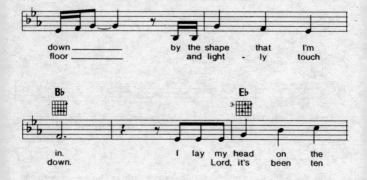

in.
down.

I lay my head on the
Lord, it's been ten

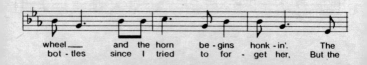

wheel ___ and the horn be - gins honk - in'. The
bot - tles since I tried to for - get her, But the

whole neigh - bor - hood   knows I'm home drunk a-
mem - 'ry still ling - ers   ly - in' here on the

gain.
ground. }   And if drink - in' don't

kill   me, _____   her mem - ory

will. __   I can't hold on much

long - er. _____   The way __   I

Eb

fe - el.   With the blood from my

Ab   Eb

bo - d - y, ___ I could start my own

Ab

still.   And if drink - in' don't

Eb   Bb

kill   me ___   her mem - ory

1. Eb   2. Eb

will. ___   These   will. ___

JAMBALAYA
(ON THE BAYOU)
Words & Music by HANK WILLIAMS

Moderately

Good - bye, Joe, me got-ta go, me oh
daux, Fon - tain - eaux, the place is

my oh _____ Me got-ta go pole the
buzz - in' _____ Kin - folk _____ come to see Y -

pi - rogue down the bay-ou _____ My Y -
vonne _____ by the doz - en _____ Dress in

vonne, the sweet - est one, me oh
style and go hog wild, me oh

my oh _____ Son of a gun, we'll have big
my oh _____ Son of a gun, we'll have big

fun   on   the   bay - ou ____
fun   on   the   bay - ou ____

____ { Jam - ba - la - ya and a craw - fish

pie   and fil - let   gum - bo ____

____ 'Cause to - night I'm gon - na

see my ma cher a - mi - o ____

Pick gui - tar, fill fruit

jar and be gay - o

Son of a gun, we'll have big

fun on the bay - ou thi - bo -

bay - ou

I'M SO LONESOME I COULD CRY

Words & Music by HANK WILLIAMS

night _____ so long   When time _____ goes
fall - ing star   Lights up _____ a

F7

crawl - ing by. _____   The
pur - ple sky. _____   And

Bb   **F**

moon   just   went   be - hind   a
as   I   won - der   where   you

C7

cloud   To __ hide   its   face   and __
are   I'm so   lone - some   I   could __

1 **F**   **2** **F**

cry _____   Did you   cry

IT'S NOW OR NEVER

Words & Music by AARON SCHROEDER & WALLY GOLD

It's now or nev-er; _____ come hold me tight.

Kiss me, my dar-lin'; _____ be mine to-night. ___

___ To-mor-row _____ will be too late. _____

___ It's now or nev-er; _____ my love won't wait

___ When I first
Just like a ___ my love won't wait. _____

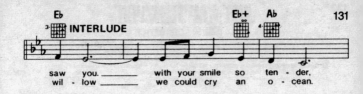

INTERLUDE

saw you. _____ with your smile so ten-der,
wil-low _____ we could cry an o-cean.

My heart was cap-tured; _____ my soul sur-
If we lost true love _____ and sweet de-

Tacet

ren-dered. I've spent a life-time _____
vo-tion. Your lips ex-cite me; _____

_____ wait-ing for the right time. Now that you're
_____ let your arms in-vite me. For who knows

Third time
Tacet D.S. al Fine

near the time is here at last. _____ ⎫ It's now or
when we'll meet a-gain this way. _____ ⎭

JUST A LITTLE LOVIN'
(WILL GO A LONG WAY)
Words & Music by ZEKE CLEMENTS & EDDY ARNOLD

Ev - er since that time be-gan___ love has ruled the
Don't be - lieve you real-ly know___ how much I love

world, E - ven A - dam set the pace___ and
you, If you did you'd come on back___ and

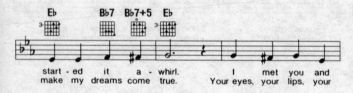

start - ed it a - whirl. I met you and
make my dreams come true. Your eyes, your lips, your

now I know___ that you're the one for me,
lov - ing kiss - es seem to lin - ger yet,

Come on back and you will plain - ly see: ___
I'll for - give but please, don't you for - get: ___

KISS AN ANGEL GOOD MORNIN'
By BEN PETERS

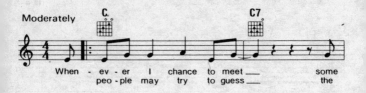

When- ev- er I chance to meet ___ some the
peo- ple may try to guess ___ the

old friends ___ on ___ the street, ___ They
se- cret of hap- pi- ness, ___ But

won- der how does a man ___ get to be this way.___
some of them nev- er learn ___ it's a sim- ple thing.___

I've
The

al - ways got a smil - in' ___ face ___
se - cret I'm ___ speak - in' ___ of

is a

an - y - time and an - y - place, ___
wom - an and a man in ___ love. ___

And
And the

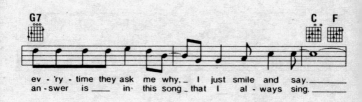

ev - 'ry - time they ask me why, ___ I just smile and say. ___
an - swer is ___ in this song ___ that I al - ways sing. ___

Tacet

___ You've got to

kiss an an - gel good morn - in'

and

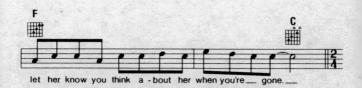

let her know you think a - bout her when you're ___ gone. ___

Kiss an an - gel good morn -

- in'   and love her like the dev - il when you

To Coda

get back home.___   Well

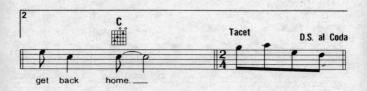

get back   home.___

D.S. al Coda

get back   home. _____

LORD MR. FORD

Words & Music by DICK FELLER

Briskly **(Recitation accompaniment)**

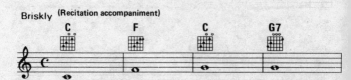

138

C   F   C   G7   C   G7

F   C   A7   G7   C   F

C   G7   C   **CHORUS**   G7

Well, Lord,   Mr. __ Ford,   I just

F7   C

wish that you could see   what your sim-ple horse-less car-riage has be-

G7   C   F

come. *Recite: Well, it seems your contribution to man, to say the least, got out of hand.*
2. Recite: Well, this world was once a garden spot, but now it's one big parkin' lot.

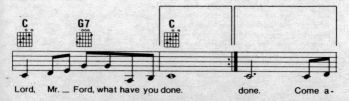

C   G7   C

Lord,   Mr. __ Ford, what have you done.   done.   Come a-

way   with   me,   Lu - cille,   in   my

D7   G7   C

smok - in'   chok - in'   au - to - mo - bile.

RECITATION

Now I'm not a man to point or judge, to bury a will or hold a grudge
But I think it's time I said a few choice words
About that demon, the automobile, a metal monster with the polyglass wheels
The end result of a dream of Henry Ford
Sure, I've got a car that's mine alone, that me and finance company own
A ready made pile of manufactured grief
If I'm not out of gas in the pouring rain, I'm changin' a flat in a hurricane
And I once spent three days lost on a clover-leaf
Well, it's not just the smoke or the graffic jam, that makes me the bitter fool I am
But that four wheel buggy is dollarin' me to death
For gas and oil and fluids and grease, and wires and tires, and anti-freeze
And them accessories, well that's something else
You can get stereo tape and color T.V. back seat bar and reclinin' seats
On top of those easy monthly payments
I figure that over a period of time, this four-thousand dollar car of mine
Cost seventeen-thousand dollars and fifty cents   (Chorus)

RECITATION 2

Now the average American father and mother own one whole car and half of another
And I'll bet that half of a car is a bitch to drive
But the thing that amazes me, I guess, is the way we measure a man's success
By the kind of automobile that he can buy
Well, it'r red light, green light, traffic cop, right turn, no turn, must turn, stop
Get out the credit card, it's time for gas
All the cars in the world placed end to end would reach to the moon and back again
And there'd probably be some fool pull out to pass;
Well, Lord, Mr. Ford, I just wish that you could see
   what your simple horseless carriage has become
Oh, how I yearn for the good old days, without that carbon dioxide haze
A-hangin' over that roar on the interstates
Well, if the Lord that made the moon and stars
   would'a meant for me and you to have cars
He'd a-seen that we were born with a parkin' space;   (Chorus)

I'M SORRY

Words and Music by RONNIE SELF and DUB ALBRITTEN

Slowly

I'm sor-ry, so sor-ry

That I was ___ such a fool. ___

I did-n't know ___ love could be so

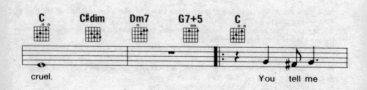

cruel. You tell me

mis-takes ___ are part of ___ be-ing young. ___ But

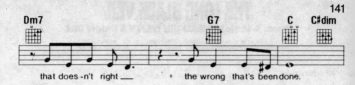

that does-n't right ___ the wrong that's been done.

I'm sor-ry, so sor-ry;

Please ac-cept my ___ a-pol-o-gy, ___ But

love is ___ blind ___ and I was too blind to

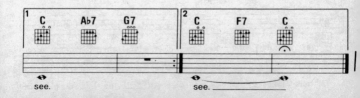

see. see. ___

THE LONG BLACK VEIL

Words & Music by MARIJOHN WILKIN & DANNY DILL

MAKE THE WORLD GO AWAY
By HANK COCHRAN

Do you re-mem-ber when you loved me
hurt you,

be-fore the world took me a-stray?
I'll make it up ___ day by day.

If you do, ___ then for-give me,
Just say you love me like you used to,

And make the world go a-way. ___
And make the world go a-way. ___

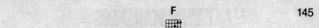

Make the world go a - way,

and get it off ___ my ___ shoul - ders,

say the things you used to say,

and make the world ___ go a - way. ___

___ I'm sor - ry if I

PAPER MANSIONS

Words & Music by TED HARRIS

1. You paint the nic-est fu-tures of

a-ny-one I know You al-ways leave me hold-ing on to

pret-ty words that glow You've built a thous-and

man-sions out of dreams that seemed so strong But they're

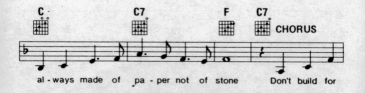

al-ways made of pa-per not of stone Don't build for

me _____ no pa - per man - sions   that I can

ne - ver call my own   For love can't

live _____ in pa - per man - sions   that on - ly

stand _____ un - til you've gone.   2. You've

2. (You've) always been a dreamer dear and I'm a dreamer too
   But I guess I've had too many of the kind that don't come true
   So don't build me no mansions with paper walls so thin
   That only stand until you leave again. (To Chorus)

IT TURNS ME INSIDE OUT

Words & Music by JAN CRUTCHFIELD

Moderately Slow

In a way I'm glad it's o - ver, e - ven
way I guess it's bet - ter, e - ven

though it's gon - na hurt me once you're gone.
though there's noth - in' good a - bout good - bye.

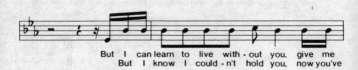

But I can learn to live with - out you, give me
But I know I could - n't hold you, now you've

time and I can make it on my own.
found new wings and you need room to fly.

Lov - in' you to me came eas - y, now
It's for sure I'm gon - na miss you, but I

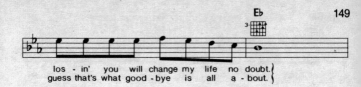

los - in' you will change my life no doubt.
guess that's what good - bye is all a - bout.

In a way I'm glad it's o - ver, in a-

noth - er way___ it turns me in - side

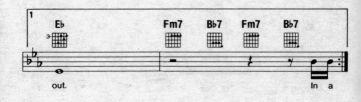

out. In a

out. On the

150

Gm **Ab**

one hand I know I'll be bet-ter off once you've gone____ But I

Eb **Bb7**

find _____ a lot of heart-aches on the

Eb **Gm**

oth-er. _____ And I can't say I'll look for-ward to those

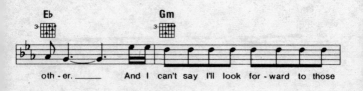

Ab

nights _____ I'll be a-lone_____ and I

Eb **Bb7** **Eb**

won-der will there ev-er be a-noth-er ____ 'Cause lov-in'

Ab

you to me came eas - y, now los - in' you will change my life no

Eb

doubt. In a

Gm7

way I'm glad it's o - ver, in a -

Fm7   Bb7

noth - er way___ it turns me in - side

1. Eb

out. In a

2. Eb

out.

BYE BYE, LOVE

Words & Music by FELICE BRYANT & BOUDLEAUX BRYANT

Moderately Fast
VERSE

There goes my ba - by ___ with some - one new;
I'm through with ro - mance, ___ I'm through with love ___

___ She sure looks hap - py; ___ I sure am blue;
___ I'm through with count - ing ___ the stars a - bove; ___

___ She was my ba - by ___ till he stepped
And here's the rea - son ___ that I'm so

in; ___ Good - bye to ro - mance ___
free: ___ My lov - in' ba - by ___

___ that might have been; ___ }
___ is through with me; ___ }   Bye   bye

CHORUS

love: Bye   bye,   hap - pi - ness;___   Hel - lo

lone - li - ness___   I   think   I'm   gon - na   cry; ___

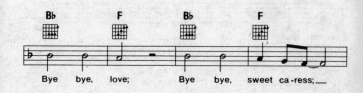

Bye   bye,   love;   Bye   bye,   sweet ca - ress;___

Hel - lo   emp - ti - ness;___   I   feel   like   I   could die___

___   Bye   bye,   my   love,   bye   bye.   bye.

RUBY, DON'T TAKE YOUR LOVE TO TOWN
Words & Music by MEL TILLIS

Moderately

You have paint - ed up your lips and rolled and
hard to love a man whose legs are
leav - ing now 'cause I just heard the

curled your tint - ed hair. _____ And the
bent and par - a - lized _____
slam - ming of a door _____ The

Ru - by, are you con - tem - plat - ing go - ing out some-
wants and the needs of a wo - man your age. Ru - by, I re - a -
way I know I've heard it slam one hun - dred times be-

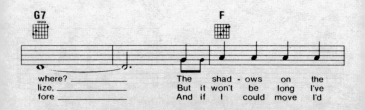

where? _____
lize, _____ The shad - ows on the
fore, _____ But it won't be long I've
And if I could move I'd

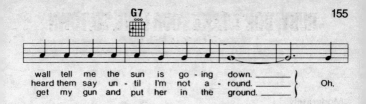

G7

wall tell me the sun is go - ing down. _____
heard them say un - til I'm not a - round. _____
get my gun and put her in the ground. _____ } Oh,

C   F

Ru _____ by, _____ Don't

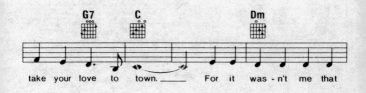

G7   C   Dm

take your love to town. _____ For it was - n't me that

F   C

start - ed that old cra - zy As - ia war, _____ But

Dm   F   G7

I was proud to go and do my pa - tri - ot - ic chores. _____

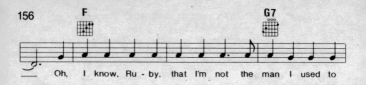

Oh, I know, Ru-by, that I'm not the man I used to

be. ___ But, Ru

by, ___ I still need your com - pa - ny. ___

It's
She's ny ___ for God's sake turn a-

round, don't take your love to town. ___

SATIN SHEETS

Words & Music by JOHN E. VOLINKATY

Moderately Slow

Sat-in sheets to lie on, Sat-in pil-lows to

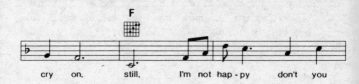

cry on, still, I'm not hap-py don't you

see. _____ Big long

Cad-il-lacs, ____ tail-or mades up-on my back,__

Still I want you to set ___ me free. _____

Verse

F

I've found an - oth - er man _____

Bb

who can give more than you can, _ though you've

F

giv - en me ev - 'ry - thing mon - ey can

C7

buy. _____

F

But your mon - ey can't hold me tight ___ like

he does _____ on a long, long night. _____

You know _____ you did-n't keep me sat - is -

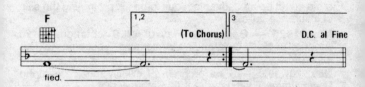

1,2 (To Chorus) **3** D.C. al Fine

fied. _____

ADDITIONAL VERSES

2. We've been through thick and thin together
   Braved the fair and stormy weather
   We've had all the hard times, you and I.
   And now that I'm a big success
   You called today and you confessed
   And told me things that made me want to die.

3. You told me there's another woman
   Who can give more than I can,
   And I've given ev'rything that cash will buy.
   You can't buy me a peaceful night
   With loving arms around me tight
   And you're too busy to notice the hurt in my eyes.

THE GRAND OLE OPRY...
HOW IT ALL BEGAN

Oct. 5, 1925 — WSM* opened on the fifth floor of the National Life building. Edwin Craig, Vice-President of National Life & Accident Insurance Company, persuaded the founders that radio could be an "advantageous force" in promoting the sale of insurance policies.

Nov. 1925 — George D. Hay of WLS Chicago, voted "America's Most Outstanding Announcer," becomes a D.J. for WSM.

Nov. 28, 1925 — First program of hillbilly music, featuring Uncle Jimmy Thompson — 8:00 Saturday night.

1927 — Creation of the name "Grand Ole Opry." "For the past half hour, we have been listening to music taken largely from Grand Opera." "But from now on, we will present the Grand Ole Opry." (George D. Hay)

1927 — Increased power to 5,000 watts and became affiliated with the National Broadcasting Company.

1932 — Acquired a clear channel frequency and increased power to 50,000 watts.

1934 — Opry moved to the Hillsboro Theater, show is divided into 15-minute segments, and segments are sold to advertisers. First advertiser — "Crazy Water Crystals."

1936 — Opry moved to The Dixie Tabernacle, "sawdust-floored religious revival house" with 2000 bench seats.

1938 — Crazy Tennesseans (Roy Acuff) came to the Grand Ole Opry. Name changed to Smoky Mountain Boys.

1939 — Blue Grass Boys (Bill Monroe) join Opry.

July 1939 — Opry moved from Dixie Tabernacle to War Memorial Auditorium. Admission fee of a quarter was instituted.

Oct. 1939 — Prince Albert Smoking Tobacco (R.J. Reynolds Co.) sponsored a 30-minute network broadcast of the Opry. These stations were scattered all the way from the Southeastern zone to the West Coast.

Spring 1940 — GRAND OLE OPRY — First movie featuring the Opry, shot in Hollywood in 2 weeks.

1940 — First major tent show — Jamup and Honey.

1942 — Roy Acuff and Fred Rose formed Acuff-Rose Publishing.

Jan. 1943 — Ralston Purina Company began sponsoring a network broadcast of an Opry half-hour, feeding it to stations in the South and Southwest.

Oct. 1943 — NBC began carrying the Prince Albert half-hour on the entire coast-to-coast network of more than 125 stations.

1943 — The state of Tennessee evicted the Opry from the War Memorial Auditorium and moved it to the Ryman Auditorium.

1948 — One of the first national radio surveys ever made — WSM was reaching a total of 10 million homes at least once a week.

1949 — The Friday-night Opry show was born.

1950 — Grand Ole Opry's first quarter-century of existence. The concept of the showcase of stars was fully formed.

1951 — Radio was no longer in the vanguard of the communications industry. The popularity of television was rising.

1953 — Attendance at the Opry was beginning to sag noticeably.

1954 — Country Music Disc Jockeys Association formed to try to gain general radio acceptance of their kind of music. Disc Jockeys Association became the Country Music Association.

1955 — Attendance stabilized at acceptable levels.

1971 — First time in history the Opry's attendance rose above 400,000.

1974 — Grand Ole Opry moved into the new Opry House at Opryland.

*WSM call letters originated from the motto of the National Life & Accident Insurance Company – "We Shield Millions."

OPRYLAND

This 120-acre musical theme park features a dozen live musical productions, twenty rides and adventures, plus shops, restaurants, games and the Roy Acuff Museum.

CRAZY

Words & Music by WILLIE NELSON

Light and carefree

Cra - zy, __ Cra - zy for feel - in' so lone - ly; __

I'm cra - zy, __ Cra - zy for feel - in' so

blue. I knew __ you'd love me as long as you

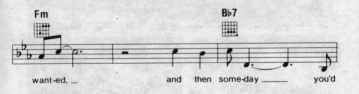

want - ed, __ and then some - day _____ you'd

leave me for some - bod - y new.

Wor-ry, ___ why do I let my-self wor-ry; ___

Won-d'rin' ___ what in the world did I do.

Cra-zy ___ for think-ing that my love could

hold you, ___ I'm cra-zy for try-in',

Cra-zy for cry-in' and I'm cra-zy for lov-in' you.

CRYSTAL CHANDELIERS

Words & Music by TED HARRIS

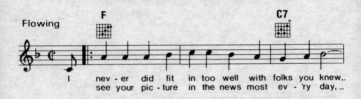

Flowing

I nev-er did fit in too well with folks you knew,_
see your pic-ture in the news most ev-'ry day,_

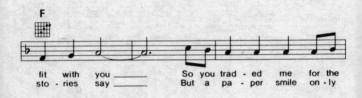

___ It was plain to see that the likes of me did-n't
___ You're the chos-en girl of the soc-ial world, so the

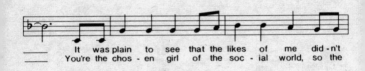

fit with you ___ So you trad-ed me for the
sto-ries say ___ But a pa-per smile on-ly

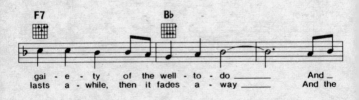

gai-e-ty of the well-to-do ___ And _
lasts a-while, then it fades a-way ___ And the

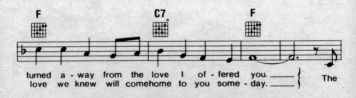

turned a-way from the love I of-fered you. ___ The
love we knew will comehome to you some-day. ___ The

crys - tal chan - de - liers light up the paint - ings on your

wall, The mar - ble stat - u - ettes are stand - ing state - ly in the

hall. __ But will the time - ly crowd that has you laugh - ing loud help you

dry your tears _____ when the new wears off of your

crys - tal chan - de - liers. _____ I __

DADDY SANG BASS

Words & Music by CARL PERKINS

Moderately

Dad-dy sang bass, ma-ma sang ten-or, me and lit-tle

bro-ther would join right in there; Sing-in' seems to

help a trou-bled soul. _____ One of these days and it won't be

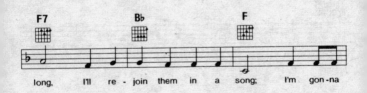

long, I'll re-join them in a song; I'm gon-na

join the fam-'ly cir-cle at the throne. _____ No, the

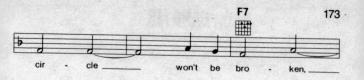

cir - cle _____ won't be bro - ken, _____

_____ Bye and bye, Lord, bye and bye. _____

_____ Dad - dy'll sing bass, ma - ma'll sing ten - or, me and lit - tle

bro - ther will join right in there in the sky, Lord ___

in the sky. _____

DANG ME
By ROGER MILLER

Well, here I sit high gettin' ideas, Ain't
Just sittin' round drinkin' with the rest of the guys,___
They say roses are red and violets are purple,___

nothin' but a fool would live like this
six rounds bought and I bought five
sugar's sweet and so is maple syruple, Well

Out all night and runnin' wild My
Spent the groceries and half the rent, I
I'm the seventh out of seven sons, My

wom-an sit-tin' home with a month old child.___
lack four-teen dol-lars hav-in' twenty sev-en cents.
pap-py was a pis-tol, I'm a son-of-a-gun.___

Dang me,   dang me,   they

ought-ta take a rope and hang me

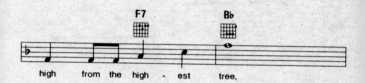

high from the high - est tree,

Wom-an, would you weep for me!

1,2

3

HONEY

Words & Music by BOBBY RUSSELL

See the tree how big it's grown, but
Then the first snow came and she ran

friend, it has-n't been too long, it was-n't big.
out to brush the snow away so it would-n't die. I Came

laughed at her and she got mad, the first day that she plant-ed it was
run-nin' in — all ex-cit-ed, slipped and al-most hurt her-self I

just a twig.
laughed 'til I cried

And Hon-ey, I

miss you, and I'm be-ing good. —

And I'd love to be with you   if on -ly I

could   She   could. _____

3. She was always young at heart,
   kinda dumb and kinda smart and I loved her so.
   I surprised her with a puppy;
   kept me up all Christmas eve two years ago.

4. And it would sure embarrass her
   when I came home from working late 'cause I would know
   That she'd been sittin' there and cryin'
   over some sad and silly late, late show.

CHORUS

5. She wrecked the car and she was sad
   and so afraid that I'd be mad, but what the heck.
   Tho' I pretended hard to be, guess you could say
   she saw through me and hugged my neck.

6. I came home unexpectedly and
   found her crying needlessly in the middle of the day,
   And it was in the early Spring
   when flowers bloom and robins sing she went away.

7. Yes, one day while I wasn't home
   while she was there and all alone the angels came.
   Now all I have is memories of Honey,
   and I wake up nights and call her name.

8. Now my life's an empty stage
   where Honey lived and Honey played and love grew up.
   A small cloud passes overhead and
   cries down in the flower bed that Honey loved.

CHORUS

I LOVE
By TOM T. HALL

Moderately Slow

I love lit-tle ba-by ducks, old — pick-up trucks,
I love o-pen hon-est smiles, kiss-es from a child,

slow mov-in' trains— and rain. I love
toma-toes on a vine and onions. I love

lit-tle coun-try streams, sleep with-out dreams,
win-ners when they cry, losers when they try,

Sun-day School in May— and hay.
Mu-sic when it's good — and life.

And

To Next Strain

I love you, too.

I WALK THE LINE

Words & Music by JOHNNY CASH

Moderately Bright

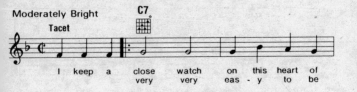

I keep a close watch on this heart of
very very eas-y to be

mine. I keep my eyes wide
true. I find my-self alone

o - pen all the time. I keep the
when each day is through. Yes, I'll ad -

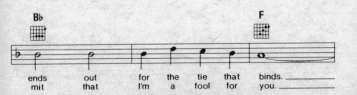

ends out for the tie that binds.
mit that I'm a fool for you.

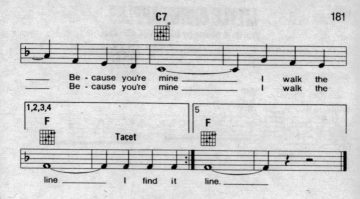

C7

Be - cause you're mine _____ I walk the
Be - cause you're mine _____ I walk the

1,2,3,4

F

Tacet

5

F

line _____ I find it

line. _____

3. As sure as night is dark and day is light,
   I keep you on my mind both day and night.
   And happiness I've known proves that it's right.
   Because you're mine I Walk The Line.

4. You've got a way to keep me on your side.
   You give me cause for love that I can't hide.
   For you I know I'd even try to turn the tide.
   Because you're mine I Walk The Line.

5. I keep a close watch on this heart of mine.
   I keep my eyes wide open all the time.
   I keep the ends out for the tie that binds.
   Because you're mine I Walk The Line.

LITTLE GREEN APPLES

Words & Music by BOBBY RUSSELL

Rather Slowly

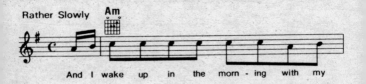

And I wake up in the morn-ing with my

hair down in my eyes and she says "Hi."___

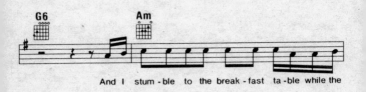

And I stum-ble to the break-fast ta-ble while the

kids are go-ing off to school, "Good-bye."___

And she reach - es out an' takes my hand;
she drops what she's do - in' and

squeez - es it, says "How you feel - in', Hon?   And I
hur - ries down to meet me and I'm always late   But __

look a - cross at smil - ing lips that warm my heart and see my morn - ing
she sits wait - ing pa - tient - ly and smiles when she first sees me 'cause she's

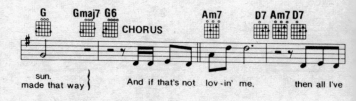

CHORUS

sun.
made that way }   And if that's not lov - in' me,   then all I've

got to say: { God did - n't make lit - tle green ap - ples and
                     { God did - n't make lit - tle green ap - ples and

Am

it don't rain in In - dian - ap - 'lis in the sum - mer - time. ___
it don't snow in Min - ne - ap - 'lis when the win - ter comes. ___

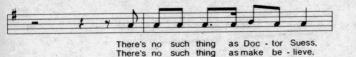

There's no such thing as Doc - tor Suess,
There's no such thing as make be - lieve.

G

Dis - ney - land and Moth - er Goose is no nurs - 'ry rhyme. ___
pup - py dogs and au - tumn leaves and ___ B. B. guns. ___

God did - n't make ___ lit - tle green ap - ples and

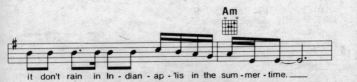

Am

it don't rain in In - dian - ap - 'lis in the sum - mer - time. ___

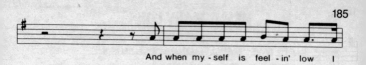

And when my-self is feel-in' low I

think a-bout her face a-glow to ease my mind. Some-

times I call her up at home know-ing she's bus-y ___

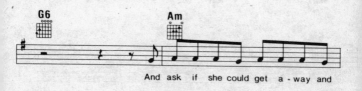

And ask if she could get a-way and

meet me ___ and grab a bite to eat. ___ And

D.S. and Fade
on Chorus

HELLO MARY LOU
(GOODBYE HEART)
By CAVET MANGIARACINA & GENE PITNEY

You passed me by one sun-ny day ___ Be-
(I) saw your lips I heard your voice Be-

Flashed those big brown eyes my way and oo I want-ed
lieve me I just had no choice, wild hors-es could-n't

you for-ev-er-more. ___ Now I'm not one that
make me stay a-way. ___ I thought a-bout a

gets a-round, I swear my feet stuck to the ground, And
moon-lit night, My arms a-bout you good an' tight, That's

though I nev-er did meet you be-fore. ___ I said "Hel-
all I had to see for me to say. ___

CHORUS

lo Ma - ry Lou Good-bye heart Sweet

Ma - ry Lou I'm so in love with you. _____ I

knew Ma - ry Lou We'd nev - er

part so hel - lo Ma - ry Lou Good-bye

heart." _____ I | heart." _____

GOOD OLE BOYS LIKE ME

Words & Music by BOB MCDILL

When I was a kid, Un-cle Re-
no-thing makes a sound

-mus he put me to bed
in the night like the wind does.

with a pic-ture of Stone-wall Jack-
But you ain't a-fraid if you're

-son a-bove my head.
washed in the blood like I was.

Then Dad-dy came in to kiss his
The smell of Cape Jas -mine thru the

lit - tle man   with gin on his breath___ and a Bi - ble
win - dow screen.   John R. and the ___ wolf-man kept me

in   his   hand.   And he talked a - bout honor and
com - pan - y   by the light of the ra - di - o   by___

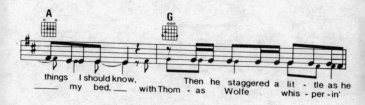

things I should know,   Then he staggered a lit - tle as he
___ my bed, ___ with Thom - as Wolfe whis - per - in'

went out the door. ___   And   I
in ___ my head. ___

CHORUS

still   hear   the   soft ___   sou - thern   wind ___

in the live _ oak trees._

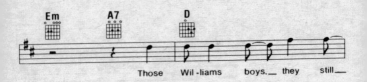

Those Wil-liams boys._ they still_

_ mean a lot _ to _ me _ Hank and Ten-

-nes-see. I guess we're all _ gon-na be _

what we're gon-na be. _

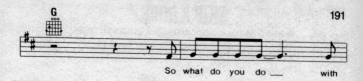

So what do you do ___ with

good ole boys ___ like me.

Well
When

Verse 3. When I was in school, I ran with a kid down the street
And I watched him burn himself up on Bourbon and speed
But I was smarter than most and I could choose
Learned to talk like the man on the six o'-clock news
When I was eighteen, Lord I hit the road
But it don't seem to matter how far I go (Chorus)

SKIP A ROPE

Words & Music by JACK MORAN & GLENN D. TUBB

Skip a rope, skip a rope!

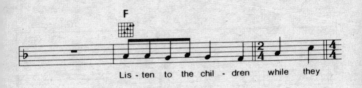

Lis-ten to the chil-dren while they

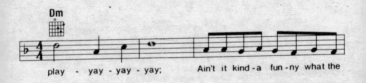

play - yay - yay - yay; Ain't it kind-a fun-ny what the

chil - dren say; _____ They say "We're

gon - na have an-oth-er lit-tle ba - by in the

fall. _____ I guess ma-ma and dad-dy weren't

(Repeat as many times as necessary)

fight-in' af-ter all. Skip a rope;

To Narration

NARRATION

(Lady) You shouldn't say that! (Man) Say what?
Skip A Rope? That's the name of the song, lady.
OK, I'll do the one about the income tax man.

2.(Sing)

The man came to see us about our income tax,
Said we're gonna get some money back,
Daddy's sorta grinning, somethin's on his mind,
He sent the income tax man a valentine.
Skip A Rope, Skip A Rope,
Oh, listen to the children while they play-yay-yay-yay,
Uh-I forgot what I'm suppose to say.

NARRATION

(Other Person) Skip A Rope! Got a joke?
Skip A Rope you dope! Tell a joke about a rope? OK.
You hear the one about the near sighted rope that fell in
love with a snake?
Oh, you messed up the punch line! Where's the punch line,
I ain't even seen a punch bowl. You know I skip a lot.
You see the doctor gave me these pills and he said take one
a day for three days running and then skip a day,
And this is my day to skip.
I used to skip a well rope. I used to skip a sick rope;
Heck, I even tried to smoke one of those one time.

(Sing)

Skip the jokes, thanks a lot, skip the jokes.
Oh, listen to the children while they play. (Fade out)

AMANDA
Words & Music by BOB MCDILL

At the hair on your shoul - ders and the
Now___ I'm crowd - ing thir - ty and

age in your___ eyes. }
still wear - in' jeans. }

A -

man - da _____

light of my _____ life _____

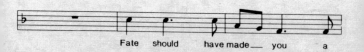

Fate should have made___ you a

gen - tle - man's wife.____ A -

man - da ____ light of my ____

life ____ Fate should have

made ____ you a gen - tle - man's wife.

Well the wife. ____

SOMEBODY'S KNOCKIN'

Words & Music by ED PENNEY & JERRY GILLESPIE

Moderately

Some-bod-y's knock-in'   should I let him in _____

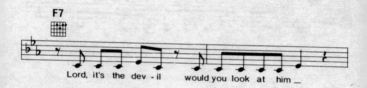

Lord, it's the dev-il   would you look at him _

I've heard a-bout him   But   I nev-er dreamed _____

he'd have blue eyes and blue jeans _____   Well, _

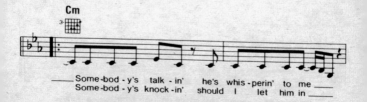

_____ Some-bod-y's talk-in'   he's whis-perin' to me _____
Some-bod-y's knock-in'   should I   let him in _____

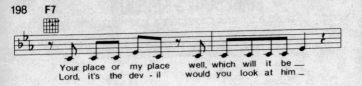

Your place or my place — well, which will it be —
Lord, it's the dev-il — would you look at him —

I'm get-tin' weak-er and he's com-in' on strong —
I've heard a-bout him — but I nev-er dreamed —

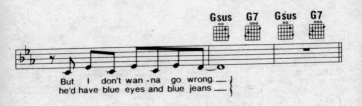

But I don't wan-na go wrong. —
he'd have blue eyes and blue jeans —

CHORUS

He must have tapped my tel-e phone line —

He must have known I'm spend-in' my time — a-lone

199

He says we'll have one hea-ven-ly night ___

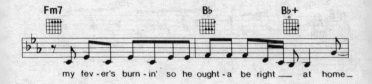

my fev-er's burn-in' so he ought-a be right ___ at home ___

Some-bod-y's knock-in'   Some-bod-y's knock-in'

Repeat and Fade

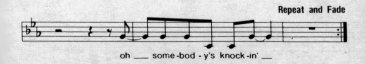

oh ___ some-bod-y's knock-in' ___

HARPER VALLEY P.T.A.

Words & Music by TOM T. HALL

I want to tell you all a sto - ry 'bout a

Har - per Val - ley wid - ow'd wife   who had a

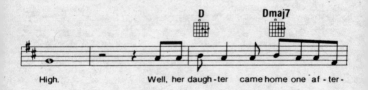

teen - age daugh - ter who at - tend - ed Har - per Val - ley Jun - ior

High.   Well, her daugh - ter came home one af - ter -

noon and did - n't e - ven stop to   play.

She said, "Mom, I got a note here from the

Har-per Val-ley P. T. A." _____

2. The note said, Mrs. Johnson, you're wearing your dresses way too high—
It's reported you've been drinking and a-runnin' 'round with men and going wild.
We don't believe you ought to be a-bringing up your little girl this way—
It was signed by the secretary, Harper Valley P.T.A.

3. Well, it happened that the P.T.A. was gonna meet that very afternoon—
They were sure surprised when Mrs. Johnson wore her mini-skirt into the room.
As she walked up to the blackboard, I still recall the words she had to say.
She said, "I'd like to address this meeting of the Harper Valley P.T.A.

4. Well, there's Bobby Taylor sittin' there and seven times he's asked me for a date.
Mrs. Taylor sure seems to use a lot of ice whenever he's away.
And Mr. Baker, can you tell us why your secretary had to leave this town?
And shouldn't widow Jones be told to keep her window shades all pulled completely down.

5. Well, Mr. Harper couldn't be here 'cause he stayed too long at Kelly's bar again.
And if you smell Shirley Thompson's breath, you'll find she's had a little nip.
Then you have the nerve to tell me you think that as a mother I'm not fit.
Well, this is just a little Peyton Place and you're all Harper Valley hypocrites.
No, I wouldn't put you on, because it really did, it happened just this way,
The day my mama socked it to the Harper Valley P.T.A.

CHUG-A-LUG
Words & Music by ROGER MILLER

Relaxed

Grape wine in a Ma - son jar,
F. F. A.
saw - dust floor

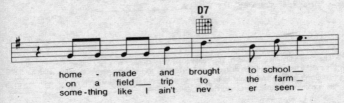

home - made and brought to school __
on a field __ trip to the farm __
some - thing like I ain't nev - er seen __

by a friend of mine __ af - ter class,
me and a friend __ sneak __ off be - hind
and I'm just __ go - ing on fif - teen

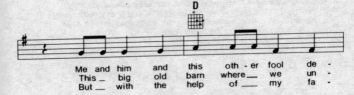

Me and him and this oth - er fool de -
This __ big old barn where __ we un -
But __ with the help of __ my fa -

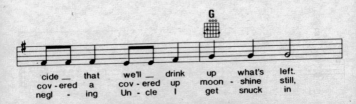

cide __ that we'll __ drink up what's left.
cov - ered a cov - ered up moon - shine still,
negl - ing Un - cle I get snuck in

ALMOST PERSUADED

Words & Music by GLENN SUTTON & BILLY SHERRILL

Last___ night all a - lone___ in a bar - room ___

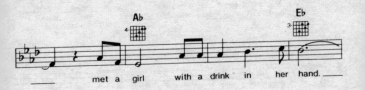

___ met a girl with a drink in her hand. ___

___ She had ru - by red lips, coal black

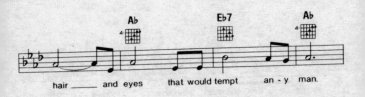

hair _____ and eyes that would tempt an - y man.

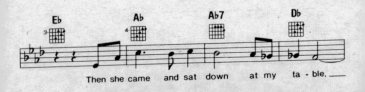

Then she came and sat down at my ta - ble, ___

and as she placed ___ her soft hands in mine. ___

I found my-self want-ing to kiss her ___

for temp-ta-tion ___ was flow-ing like wine.

And I was al-most ___ per-suad-ed ___

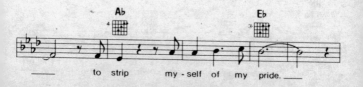

to strip my-self of my pride. ___

Al - most __ per - suad - ed __ to

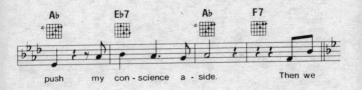

push my con - science a - side. Then we

danced and she whis - pered, "I need you!" __ "Take me a-

way __ from here and be my man." __ Then I

looked in - to her eyes and I saw it: __ The re-

flec-tion___ of my wed-ding band.___ And I was

al-most___ -per-suad-ed___ to

let strange lips lead me on.___

Al - most___ per-suad-ed___ but your

sweet love made me stop and go home.___

HEARTBREAK HOTEL

By MAE BOREN AXTON, TOMMY DURDEN & ELVIS PRESLEY

Moderate blues

Now, since my ba - by left me I've found a

new place to dwell, down at the end of Lone -ly street at

Heart - break Ho - tel. I'm so lone - ly, _____ I'm so

lone - ly, _____ I'm so lone - ly, _____ that I could

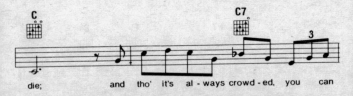

die; and tho' it's al - ways crowd - ed, you can

still find some room   for brok-en-heart-ed lov-ers to

cry there in __ the gloom and be so lone-ly, _____ oh, so

lone-ly, _____   oh, so lone-ly _____   they could

die.   The   die.
        So

2. The bell hop's tears keep flowing, the desk clerk's dressed in
   black . . . They've been so long on Lonely street,
   They never will go back . . . and they're so lonely . . .Oh, they're
   so lonely . . .they're so lonely . . . they pray to die.

3. So, if your baby leaves and you have a tale to tell,
   Just take a walk down Lonely street . . . to Heartbreak Hotel,
   Where you'll be so lonely . . . and I'll be so lonely . . . We'll be so
   lonely . . . That we could die.

HELLO WALLS

By WILLIE NELSON

With a beat

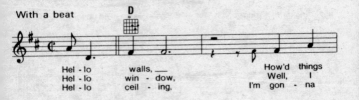

Hel - lo   walls, ___   How'd things
Hel - lo   win - dow,   Well, I
Hel - lo   ceil - ing,   I'm gon - na

go   for   you   to - day,   don't you   miss   her
see   that you're still here,   aren't you   lone - ly
stare at   you   a - while, you know   I   can't sleep.

since she   up   and walked a - way,   and I'll
since our dar - lin' dis - ap - peared, well, look
so won't you bear with me   a - while,   we   must

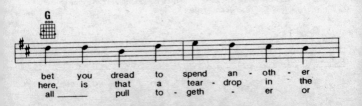

bet   you   dread   to   spend   an - oth - er
here,   is   that   a   tear - drop   in   the
all ___   pull   to - geth - er   or

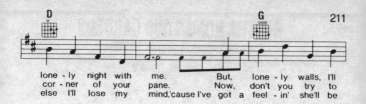

lone - ly night with me. But, lone - ly walls, I'll
cor - ner of your pane. Now, don't you try to
else I'll lose my mind, 'cause I've got a feel - in' she'll be

keep you com - pa - ny.
tell me that it's rain.
gone a long, long time.

She went a - way and left us all a - lone

the way she planned guess we'll have to learn to

get a - long with - out her if we can.

212

BETTER HOMES AND GARDENS

Words & Music by BOBBY RUSSELL

Copyright © 1969, 1983 Bibo Music Publishers c/o The Welk Music Group, Santa Monica, Calif. 90401
International copyright secured.   All rights reserved.
Used by permission.

Now, you say you're tired   of her and you've found a fas-ter
same girl that you swore awhile back, that you'd spend your whole life

life;   You're have-in' trou-ble go-in' home to her when you
thru;   And short-ly af-ter that,   didn't she hang it up for

get off work at night.   You say you're din-in'
life, to mar-ry you. Hey are you a-fraid that the boys at the

out with friends and you won't be home till late;   And
of-fice   will   no __ long-er call you "Stud?"   Have

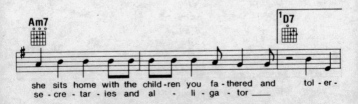

she sits home with the child-ren you fa-thered and   tol-er-
se-cre-tar-ies and al-li-ga-tor __

ates. Now, was-n't that the shoes got-ten in your

blood; You'd bet-ter mend your bet-ter homes and gar-dens,

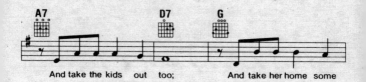

And take the kids out too; And take her home some

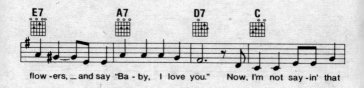

flow-ers, __ and say "Ba - by, I love you." Now, I'm not say-in' that

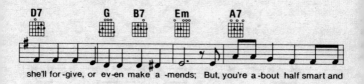

she'll for-give, or ev-en make a -mends; But, you're a-bout half smart and

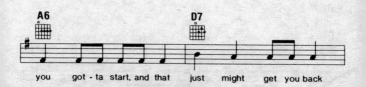

you got-ta start, and that just might get you back

in; Have -n't you heard that that door swings both ways, my friend, And

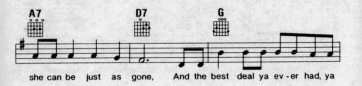

she can be just as gone, And the best deal ya ev-er had, ya

ev-er had, ya ev-er had is sit-tin' right there at home. You

say you're get-tin' caught up ear-ly, and cheat-ed out of

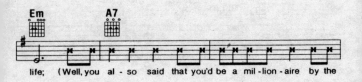

life; (Well, you al-so said that you'd be a mil-lion-aire by the

D.S. and Fade

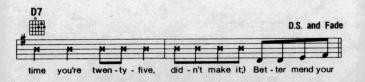

time you're twen-ty-five, did-n't make it;) Bet-ter mend your

RUNNING BEAR

By J.P. RICHARDSON

Moderately
VERSE

On the   bank   of   the   riv-er ____ stood Run-ning
swim   the rag -ing   riv-er ____   'cause the

Bear, ____   young In-dian brave.   On the
riv-er ____   was   too   wide.   He could-n't

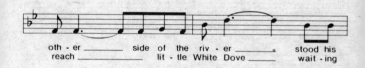

oth-er ____   side of the riv-er ____   stood his
reach ____   lit-tle White Dove ____   wait-ing

love-ly ____   In - dian maid.   Lit - tle
on ____   the other side.   In the

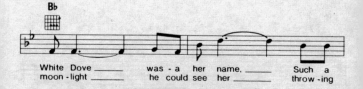

White Dove ____   was-a her name, ____   Such a
moon-light ____   he could see her ____   throw-ing

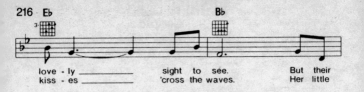

love - ly _____ sight to see. But their
kiss - es _____ 'cross the waves. Her little

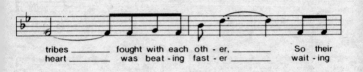

tribes _____ fought with each oth - er, So their
heart _____ was beat - ing fast - er _____ wait - ing

CHORUS
(with a beat)

love _____ could nev - er be. }
there _____ for _____ her brave. }

Run - ning

Bear loved lit - tle White Dove _____ with a

love big as the sky. Run - ning

Bear loved lit - tle White Dove _____ with a love _____ that could - n't die. _____ He could - n't die. Run - ning die. _____

3. Running Bear dove in the water.
   Little White Dove did the same
   And they swam out to each other
   Through the swirling stream they came.
   As their hands touched and their lips met
   The raging river pulled them down.
   Now they'll always be together
   In that Happy Hunting Ground.

HEARTACHES BY THE NUMBER
By HARLAN HOWARD

With a beat

VERSE

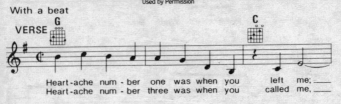

Heart-ache num-ber one was when you left me;
Heart-ache num-ber three was when you called me,

I nev-er knew that I could hurt this
and said that you were com-ing back to

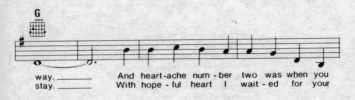

way. And heart-ache num-ber two was when you
stay. With hope-ful heart I wait-ed for your

came back a-gain; you came back and
knock on the door; I wait-ed, but you

CHORUS

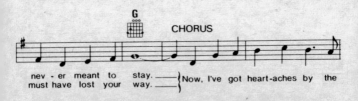

nev-er meant to stay. Now, I've got heart-aches by the
must have lost your way.

num - ber, trou - bles by the score; Ev - 'ry day you

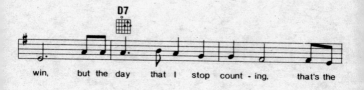

love me less, each day I love you more. ___ Yes, I've got

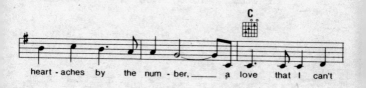

heart - aches by the num - ber, ___ a love that I can't

win, but the day that I stop count - ing, that's the

day my world will end. ___

I SAW THE LIGHT

Words & Music by HANK WILLIAMS

Moderately
VERSE

I wan-dered so aim-less life filled with
Just like a blind man I wan-dered a-

sin. I would-n't let my dear Sav-iour
long. Wor-ries and fears I claimed for my

in. ____ Then Je-sus came like a
own. ____ Then like the blind man that

strang-er in the night Praise the Lord _____
God gave back his sight Praise the Lord _____

CHORUS

I saw the light.
I saw the light.
I saw the light, _____

I saw the light, _____ No more

dark - ness, No more night _____

Now I'm so hap - py, no sor - row in

sight. _____ Praise the Lord _____

1 I saw the light. 2 I saw the light

SHUTTERS AND BOARDS

Words & Music by AUDIE MURPHY & SCOTT TURNER

Copyright © 1962 Vogue Music
This Arrangement Copyright © 1983 Vogue Music c/o The Welk Group, Santa Monca, Calif. 90401
International Copyright Secured   Made In U.S.A.   All Rights Reserved

Moderate Waltz

CHORUS

Shut - ters __ and boards, cov - er __ the

win - dows of the house ___ where we used to

live. ___ All I have left is a

heart full of sor - row. Since she

said she'd nev - er for - give. ___

1,2
To verse

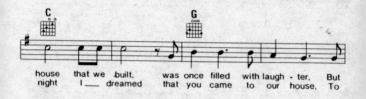

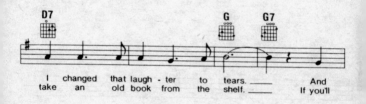

WATERLOO

Words & Music by JOHN LOUDERMILK & MARIJOHN WILKIN

My, my, ___ at Wa - ter - loo Nap - o -
I tried to hold you back, ___

___ le - on ___ did sur - ren - der. ___ Oh yeah, ___
___ but you were strong - er. ___ Oh yeah,

___ And I ___ have met ___ my des -
And now ___ it seems my on -

- ti - ny ___ in quite a sim - i - lar way. ___
- ly chance ___ is giv - in' up the fight. ___

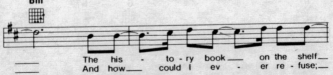

The his - to - ry book ___ on the shelf ___
And how ___ could I ev - er re - fuse; ___

is al - ways re - peat - ing it - self.

I feel like I win when I lose.

Wa - ter - loo, I

was de - feat - ed, you won the war. Wa-

- ter - loo, prom - ise to love you for - ev -

- er - more. Wa - ter - loo, could

ROOM FULL OF ROSES

Words & Music by TIM SPENCER

Moderately

If I sent a rose to you for

ev - 'ry time you made me blue.

You'd have a room full of ros - es, _____

_____ If I sent a rose of white for

ev - 'ry time I cried all night.

You'd have a room full of

ros - es, _____ And if you took the

pet - als and you tore them all a -

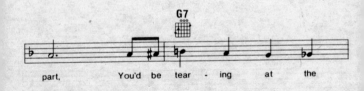

part, You'd be tear - ing at the

ros - es just the way you tore my heart.

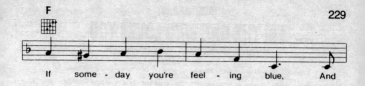

F

If some-day you're feel-ing blue, And

you could send some ros-es, too,

F#dim

Well, I don't want a room full of

Gm7 **C7** **Gm** **Gm7**

ros - es, _____ I just want my

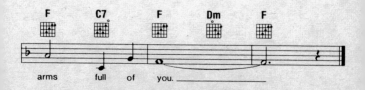

F **C7** **F** **Dm** **F**

arms full of you. _____

(REMEMBER ME)

I'M THE ONE WHO LOVES YOU

Words & Music by STUART HAMBLEN

Thoughtfully

When you're all a - lone and blue,   No one to

tell your trou - bles to,   Re - mem - ber me,   I'm the

one who loves you. _____ When this world has turned you

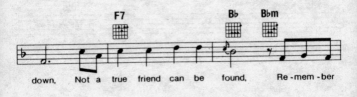

down, Not a true friend can be found,   Re - mem - ber

me,   I'm the one   who loves you. _____   And

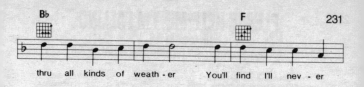

thru all kinds of weath-er You'll find I'll nev-er

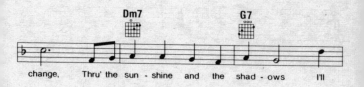

change, Thru' the sun-shine and the shad-ows I'll

al-ways be the same. We're to-geth-er right or

wrong, Where you go I'll tag a-long, Re-mem-ber

me, I'm the one who loves you. _____

PLEASE HELP ME, I'M FALLING
(In Love With You)
Words & Music by DON ROBERTSON & HAL BLAIR

Please help me, I'm fall - ing ____
oth - er ____
fall - ing ____

____ in love with ____ you.
Whose arms have grown cold.
And that would be sin.

____ Close the door to temp - ta - tion; ____
____ But I prom - ised for - ev - er ____
____ Close the door to temp - ta - tion; ____

____ Don't let me walk through. ____
____ To have and to hold. ____
____ Don't let me walk in. ____

Tacet

F

Turn a - way from me, dar - ling,
So I can nev - er be free, dear,
For I must - n't want you,

F7 Eb F7 Bb

I'm beg - ging you to.
But when I'm with you,
But, dar - ling, I do.

F

Please help me, I'm fall - ing
I know that I'm los - ing
Please help me, I'm fall - ing

C7

1,2
F

in love with you.
the strength to be true.
in love with

Tacet

3
F

I be-long to an -
Please help me, I'm you.

NOBODY LIKES SAD SONGS

Words & Music by WAYLAND HOLYFIELD & BOB McDILL

You've seen the way I en-ter-tain a crowd;

I used to pack 'em in _____ from

miles a-round; _____

And I'd play the hap-py songs that

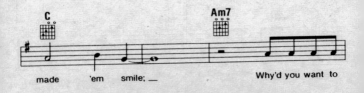

made 'em smile; _   Why'd you want to

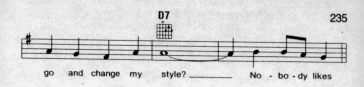

go and change my style? _____ No - bo -dy likes

sad ___ songs; The ones a - bout ___ good-byes; ___

_____ Songs a - bout bro - ken hearts ___ with

tears in your eyes; _____ No - bo - dy likes

Moderately

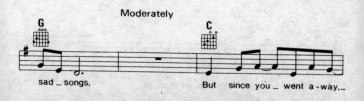

sad _ songs, But since you _ went a - way, _

236

seems like sad ___ songs are

all I can play. ___

To Coda ⊕

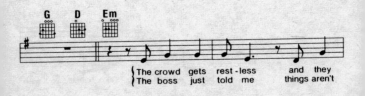

The crowd gets rest-less and they
The boss just told me things aren't

drift a - way;
go - ing well;

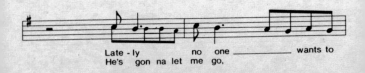

Late - ly no one _____ wants to
He's gon na let me go,

hear me play; —
I can tell; —

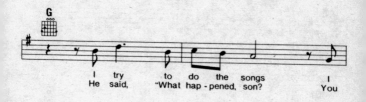

G

I try to do the songs
He said, "What hap-pened, son?

I
You

C

used to do;
had it made.

Am7   D

Ah, _____ but then I think of you; —
Why'd _____ you change the way you play?"

1
And no-bo-dy likes

2   D.S. al Coda
'Cause no-bo-dy likes

CODA   G

RAINING IN MY HEART

Words & Music by BOUDLEAUX BRYANT & FELICE BRYANT

The sun is out, the sky is blue, there's not a cloud to

spoil the view__ But it's rain - ing, Rain - ing in my heart. __

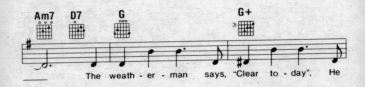

The weath - er - man says, "Clear to - day", He

does - n't know you've gone a - way__ and it's rain - ing,

Rain - ing in my heart. _____ Oh, mis - er -

239

y, mis - er - y, _____

What's gon - na be - come ___ of me. _____

___ I tell my blues they must - n't show, but

soon these tears are bound to flow ___ 'Cause it's rain - ing,

Rain - ing in my heart. _____

SAVE YOUR HEART FOR ME

Words and Music by BOB McDILL

Moderately Fast

Some of us are tak - ers, ___
I'm not one for tak - in' ___
peo - ple all a - round ___ you have

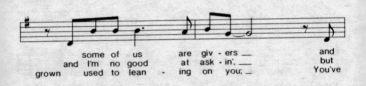

some of us are giv - ers ___ and
and I'm no good at ask - in', ___ but
grown used to lean - ing on you; ___ You've

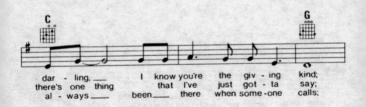

dar - ling, ___ I know you're the giv - ing kind;
there's one thing that I've just got - ta say,
al - ways ___ been ___ there when some - one calls;

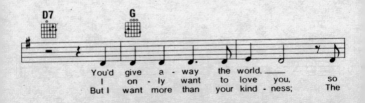

You'd give a - way the world, ___
I on - ly want to love you, so
But I want more than your kind - ness; The

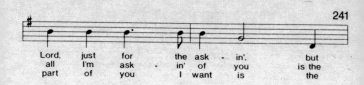

Lord, just for the ask - in', but
all I'm ask - in' of you is the
part of you I want is the

C

that's the way you are so I don't
part of you you nev - er gave a -
part of you that mat - ters most of

1 **G**

mind.

2,3 **G**

Now way.}
all.}

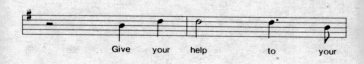

Give your help to your

mo - ther, your ad - vice to your

242

bro-ther; Your mon-ey to some beg-gar on the

street; Give your clothes to your

sis - ter, your re-spect to your dad-dy;

Give your soul to Je-sus, but save your heart___ for

To Coda D.C. al Coda CODA

me.___ Well the ___

KAW-LIGA

Words by FRED ROSE
Music by HANK WILLIAMS

Kaw - Li - ga was a wood - en In - di - an
al - ways wore his Sun - day feath - ers and

stand - ing by ___ the door ___ He
held a tom - a - hawk. ___ The

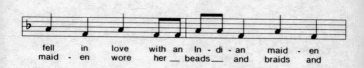

fell in love with an In - di - an maid - en
maid - en wore her ___ beads ___ and braids and

o - ver in the an - tique store. Kaw - Li - ga ___
hoped ___ some - day he'd talk. Kaw - Li - ga ___

Just
Too

stood there and nev - er let it show _____
stub - born to ev - er show a sign _____

_____ So she could nev - er an - swer "yes" or
_____ Be - cause his heart was made of knot - ty

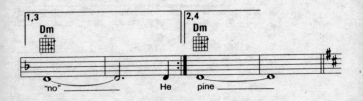

"no" _____ He pine _____

CHORUS

Poor ol' Kaw - Li - ga, he

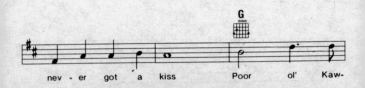

nev - er got a kiss Poor ol' Kaw-

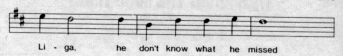

Li - ga, he don't know what he missed

D

Is it an - y won - der that his face is

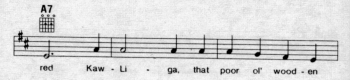

A7

red Kaw - Li - ga, that poor ol' wood - en

1. D   **2. Dm**

head _____   Kaw - head. _____

2. (Kaw)-liga was a lonely Indian, never went nowhere
   His heart was set on the Indian maiden with the coal black hair.
   Kaw-liga just stood there and never let it show so she could never
   answer "yes" or "no"

3. And then one day a wealthy customer bought the Indian maid and took
   her, oh, so far away but ol' Kaw-liga stayed.
   Kaw-liga just stands there as lonely as can be and wishes he was still
   an old pine.

TALK ABOUT THE GOOD TIMES

Words & Music by JERRY REED HUBBARD

Lively

VERSE

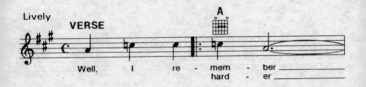

Well, I re - mem - ber ____
hard - er ____

____ when I was just chil - dren. ____
____ and the peo - ple are chang - in'. ____

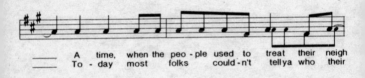

____ A time, when the peo - ple used to treat their neigh
To - day most folks could - n't tell ya who their

- bors like a fel - low man. ____
next door neigh - bors are. ____

Them all - day sing - in's
All the guns are load - ed

and them   big   prayer   meet - in's _____
the front doors   are   bolt - ed. _____

____ when a man was   proud to walk   up   and
____ Ain't this old   world takin' hate and

shake on   his   neigh - bor's hand. _____
fear   just a   lit - tle too   far? _____

CHORUS

____ Lord, you talk a - bout the good   times,
____ Let's _   talk a - bout the good   times.

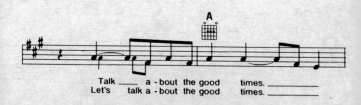

Talk ____ a - bout the good   times. _____
Let's   talk a - bout the good   times. _____

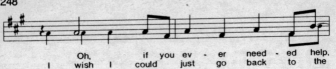

Oh,   if you ev - er need - ed help,
I wish I could just go back to the

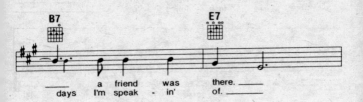

B7   E7

_____ a friend was there. _____
days I'm speak - in' of. _____

D7

Some   good neigh - bor _____
When a friend would meet you _____

A

_____ would help lift your bur - den,
_____ and a smile would greet you,

F#m   A

   and the sim - ple joys of
What this old world needs now is

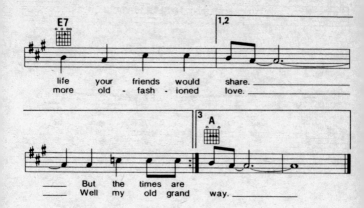

life   your   friends   would   share. _____
more   old - fash - ioned   love. _____

_____ But   the   times   are
_____ Well my   old   grand   way. _____

Verse 3. Well, my old grand daddy, God rest his soul now
      Well, we had a big long talk together the day he died
      He said, "Son this world is so full of hate and venom
      And I can't wait to leave this ol' place and rest on the other side
      (CHORUS)

Verse 4. 'Cause you talk about a good time, talk about a good time
      Well, I'm gonna see all the friends I knew in the good old days
      We'll have a big hand shakin', and sit and talk together
      Sit down by the river Jordan and sing our cares away.

BUSTED

Words & Music by HARLAN HOWARD

My bills are all due and the
went to my broth - er to a
I am no thief, but a

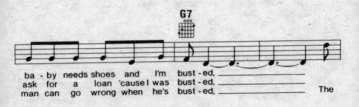

ba - by needs shoes and I'm bust - ed,
ask for a loan 'cause I was bust - ed,
man can go wrong when he's bust - ed, _____ The

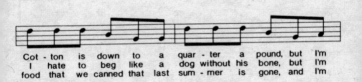

Cot - ton is down to a quar - ter a pound, but I'm
I hate to beg like a dog without his bone, but I'm
food that we canned that last sum - mer is gone, and I'm

bust - ed. _____ I got a
bust - ed. _____ My
bust - ed. _____ The

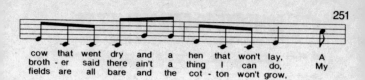

cow that went dry and a hen that won't lay,
broth-er said there ain't a thing I can do,
fields are all bare and the cot-ton won't grow,
A
My

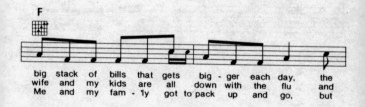

F

big stack of bills that gets big-ger each day,
wife and my kids are all down with the flu
Me and my fam-'ly got to pack up and go,
the
and
but

G7

coun-ty's gonna haul my be-long-ings a-way 'cause I'm
I was just think-in' about call-in' on you and I'm
I'll make a liv-ing, just where I don't know,'cause I'm

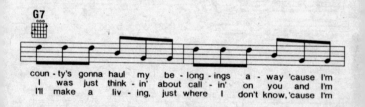

1,2 C F C F C

bust-ed. _____
bust-ed. _____
I
Well,

3 C F C F C

bust-ed. _____
(Spoken) I'm broke, no bread, I mean nothin', forget it!

SOMEONE TO GIVE MY LOVE TO

Words & Music by JERRY FOSTER & BILL RICE

Casually

I could   search   from now___   till   the   end___
I   be - lieve,   my   love.___   that you're one___

_____   of   time____
_____   of   a   kind,___

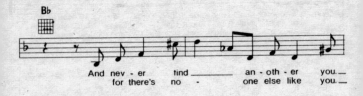

And   nev - er   find _____   an - oth - er   you.___
for there's   no -   one   else   like   you.___

I'm ___   so   glad _____   be - cause_____   I ___
You're ___   the   light ___   of   my   life, _____   so ___

know _ you're mine,_____
let ____ it shine,_____ }

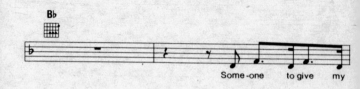

Some-one   to give   my

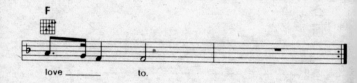

love _____   to.

I find____ hap-pi - ness _ is

lov - ing ___ you._____

254

D | **D9**

I'll __ do my best __ to make your

G | **G7**

dreams _____ come __

C7

true. _____

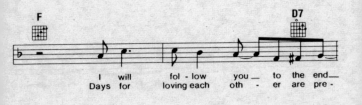

F | **D7**

I will fol - low you __ to the end__
Days for loving each oth - er are pre -

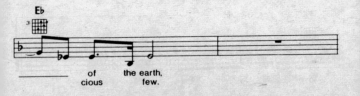

Eb

_____ of the earth,
cious few.

Bb

For my place _____ will be with _
I will spend _____ them all with _

F

_____ you. _____
_____ you. _____ I have
For as

Eb

tak - en you _____ for bet - ter or worse,
long as you want me I'll stay with you,

Bb

Some - one to give my

F

love _____ to.

WAKE UP, LITTLE SUSIE
By BOUDLEAUX BRYANT & FELICE BRYANT

Moderately Bright

Wake up, lit-tle Su - sie, _ wake up

Wake up lit - tle Su - sie, _

wake up

We've both been sound a - sleep, _
The mov - ie was - n't so hot _

Wake up, _ lit - tle Su - sie, and weep   The
It did - n't have much of a plot   We

mov - ie's o - ver, it's four o' - clock _ and we're in trou - ble
fell a - sleep, _ our goose is cooked _ our rep - u - ta - tion is

deep shot {Wake up, _ lit - tle Su - sie, _   Wake up, _ lit - tle

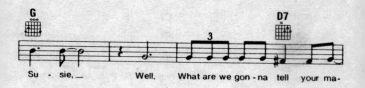

Su - sie, _   Well,   What are we gon - na tell your ma-

- ma? _   What are we gon - na tell   your Pa? _

What are we gon - na tell our friends _ when they say,   "Ooh la

la" Wake up, _ lit - tle Su - sie _   Wake up, _ lit - tle

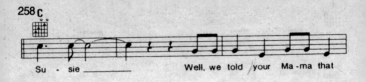

Su - sie _____ Well, we told your Ma - ma that

we'd be in by ten Well, Su - sie ba - by, looks

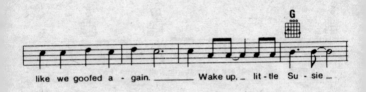

like we goofed a - gain. _____ Wake up, _ lit - tle Su - sie _

Wake up, _ lit - tle Su - sie _ We've got - ta go

home   Su - sie. _____

SAVE THE LAST DANCE FOR ME
By DOC POMUS & MORT SHUMAN

Moderately

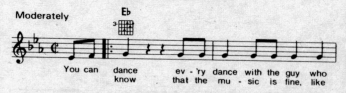

You can dance ev - 'ry dance with the guy who
know that the mu - sic is fine, like

gave you the eye; let him hold you tight. ___
spark - ling wine; ___ go and have your fun. ___
You can
Laugh and

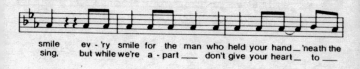

smile ev - 'ry smile for the man who held your hand ___ 'neath the
sing, but while we're a - part ___ don't give your heart ___ to ___

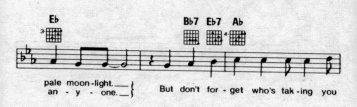

pale moon - light. ___ }
an - y - one. ___ }
But don't for - get who's tak - ing you

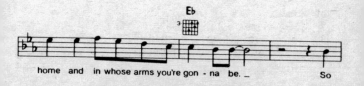

home and in whose arms you're gon - na be. ___
So

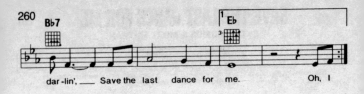

dar-lin', ___ Save the last dance for me. Oh, I

me. Ba-by, don't you know I love you so? ___

___ Can't you feel it when we touch? I will nev-er, nev-er

let you go. ___ I love you, oh, so much.

You can dance, go and car-ry on ___ till the

night is gone — and it's time to go. — If he

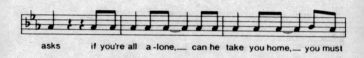

asks if you're all a-lone, — can he take you home, — you must

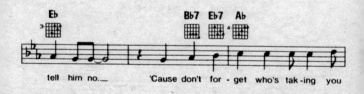

tell him no. — 'Cause don't for-get who's tak-ing you

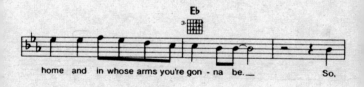

home and in whose arms you're gon-na be. — So,

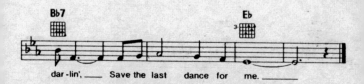

dar-lin', — Save the last dance for me. —

(HEY, WON'T YOU PLAY)
ANOTHER SOMEBODY DONE
SOMEBODY WRONG SONG

Words & Music by LARRY BUTLER & CHIPS MOMAN

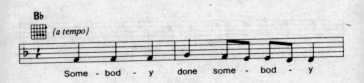

play   an-oth-er   some-bod-y

done some-bod-y wrong___ song.

And make me feel__ at home.___   while I miss my

ba - by,   while I miss   my

ba - by.   So, play,   play for

264

A **A7**

me   a   sad   mel - o - dy.   So

D **D7** **G**

sad   that   it   makes   ev -'ry - bod - y   cry. ____

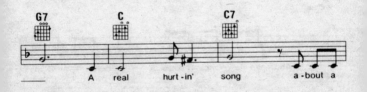

G7 **C** **C7**

____   A   real   hurt -in'   song   a - bout a

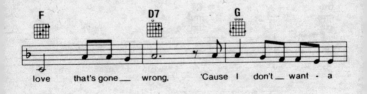

F **D7** **G**

love   that's gone ___ wrong,   'Cause I   don't ___ want - a

G7 **C** **C7**   **D.S. and Fade**

cry   all   a - long.

HEY, GOOD LOOKIN'

Words & Music by HANK WILLIAMS

Hey,   hey,   good   look - in'
(I'm)   free   and   read - y   so

What   - cha   got   cook - in'
we _____ can   go   stead - y

How's a - bout   cook - in'   some - thin' up ____ with
How's a - bout   sav - in'   all   your   time   for

me _____
me _____

Hey,   sweet   ba - by,
No   more   look - in',   I

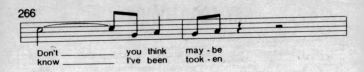

Don't _____ you think may - be
know _____ I've been took - en

D7 **G7** **C**

We could find us a brand new rec - i - pe _____
How's a - bout keep - in' stead - y com - pa - ny _____

C7 **F**

_____ I got a hot rod Ford and a
I'm gon - na throw my date book

C **F**

two dol - lar bill and I know a spot right
o - ver the fence and find me _____ one for

C **F**

o - ver the hill _____ There's so - da pop and the
five or ten cents I'll keep it 'til it's _____

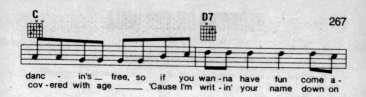

danc - in's __ free, so if you wan -na have fun come a-
cov -ered with age _____ 'Cause I'm writ - in' your name down on

long with me __ Hey, good look - in'
ev - 'ry page Hey, good look - in'

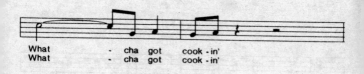

What - cha got cook - in'
What - cha got cook - in'

How's a - bout cook - in' some - thin' up __ with
How's a - bout cook - in' some - thin' up __ with

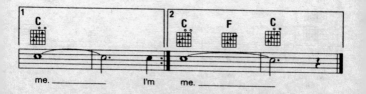

me. _____ I'm
me. _____

FLOWERS ON THE WALL

Words & Music by LEWIS DEWITT

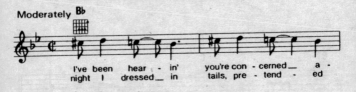

I've been hear - in' you're con - cerned__ a -
night I dressed__ in tails, pre - tend - ed

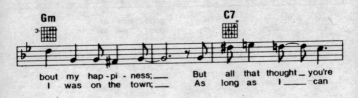

bout my hap - pi - ness;__ But all that thought__ you're
I was on the town;__ As long as I____ can

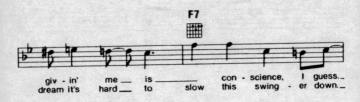

giv - in' me __ is ____ con - science, I guess..
dream it's hard__ to slow this swing - er down.__

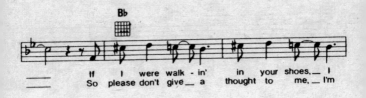

If I were walk - in' in your shoes,__ I
So please don't give__ a thought to me, __ I'm

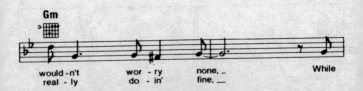

would - n't wor - ry none, __ While
real - ly do - in' fine, __

you and your friends___ are wor-ryin' 'bout me ___ I'm
You ___ can al - ways find____ me here___ and

hav - in' lots of fun. ___
hav - in' quite a time. ___ }   Count - in'

flow - ers on the wall, ___ that don't

both - er me at all, ___ Play - in'

sol - i - tare ___ till dawn___ with a

deck of fif - ty - one. ___ Smok - in'

Eb

cig - a - rettes ___ and watch - in' Cap - tain Kan - ga - roo. ___

F   Eb

___ Now don't ___ tell me, I've noth - in' to

1. F   2. F   Eb

do. ___   Last do.   Don't tell

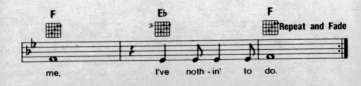

F   Eb   F Repeat and Fade

me,   I've noth - in' to do.

MY HEROES HAVE ALWAYS BEEN COWBOYS

Words & Music by SHARON VAUGHN

Moderately Slow

I grew up ___ a - dream - ing ___ of be - ing a
Cow - boys ___ are spe - cial with their own brand of

cow - boy, and lov - ing ___ the cow - boy
mi - s'ry from be - ing ___ a - lone too

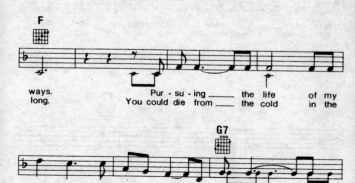

ways. Pur - su - ing ___ the life of my
long. You could die from ___ the cold in the

high - rid - in' he - roes, ___ I burned up ___ my
arms of a night - mare, ___ know - ing well that your

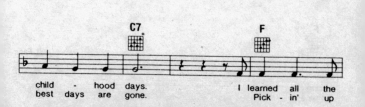

child - hood days. I learned all the
best days are gone. Pick - in' up

272

rules of a mod - ern day drift - er, don't you
hook - ers in - stead of my pen __ I let the

Bb **F**

hold on ____ to noth - in' ____ too long, Just
words of my youth fade a - way.

Bb **F**

take what ____ you need __ from the la - dies then
Old worn ____ out sad - dles and old worn out

Bb **F** **C7**

leave them with the words of a sad coun - try
mem - 'ries with no one and no place to

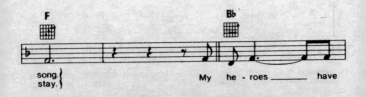

F **Bb**

song.}
stay.} My he - roes ____ have

al - ways been cow-boys,___ and they

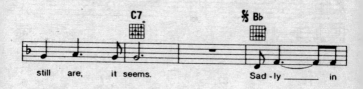

still are, it seems. Sad - ly ___ in

search of ___ and one step in back of ___ them-selves and their

slow mov - in' dreams.

dreams. dreams. ___

WHEN YOU'RE HOT, YOU'RE HOT

Words & Music by JERRY REED HUBBARD

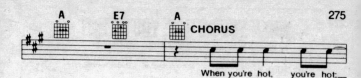

CHORUS

When you're hot, you're hot;—

— and when you're not, you're not.

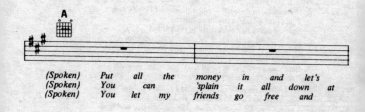

(Spoken) Put all the money in and let's
(Spoken) You can 'splain it all down at
(Spoken) You let my friends go free down and

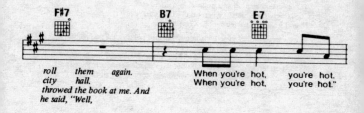

roll them again.
city hall.
throwed the book at me. And
he said, "Well,

When you're hot, you're hot.
When you're hot, you're hot."

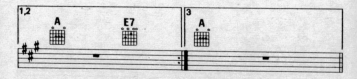

Recitation 4

Repeat and Fade (after Reciation 4)

1. Well, now me and Homer Jones and Big John Talley
   had a big crap game going back in the alley;
   and I kept rolling them sevens and winning all them pots.
   My luck was so good I could do no
   wrong, I just kept on rolling
   and controlling them bones, and finally they just threw up their
   hands and said,
   "When you're hot, you're hot!" I said, "Yeah," (To Chorus)

2. Well, now, every time I rolled them dice I'd win and
   I was just gettin' ready to roll them
   again, when I heard something behind me
   and I turned around and there was a big ole cop.
   He said, "Hello, boys," then he gave us a grin and said,
   "Looks like I'm going to have to
   haul you all in and keep all that money for evidence."
   I said, "Well, son, when you're hot, you're hot." He said, (To Chorus)

3. Well, when he took us into court I couln't believe my eyes.
   The judge was a fishing buddy that I recognized.
   I said, "Hey judge, old buddy, old pal, I'll pay you that
   hundred I owe you if you get me out of this spot".
   So he gave my friends a little fine to pay.
   He turned around and grinned at me and said,
   "Ninety days, Jerry, when you're hot, you're hot"
   and I said, "Thanks a lot". (To Chorus)

4. So I said, I'll tell you one thing judge, old buddy, old pal, if you
   wasn't wearin' that black robe, I'd take you out
   in back of this courthouse and I'd try a little of your honor on.
   You understand that you hillbilly, who's gonna collect my welfare?
   Pay for my Cadillac? What do you mean contempty of court
   - - - Judge - - - oh, Judge - - - Judgie - poo - -

YOU NEEDED ME

Words & Music by RANDY GOODRUM

278

lone a-gain___ to face the world out on my

own a-gain___ You put me high up - on a

ped - es - tal _____ so high that I ___ can al - most see___ e-

ter - ni - ty, _____ You need - ed me, _____ You

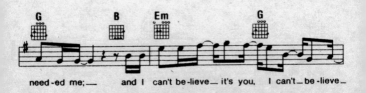

need - ed me; ___ and I can't be - lieve ___ it's you, I can't ___ be - lieve ___

_____ it's true._____ I need-ed you_____ and you were

there _____ and I'll nev-er leave Why should _____ I leave _____ I'd be_____

_____ a fool_____ 'cause I've fin-'lly found_____ some-one _____ who real - ly cares._____

_____ You held my

need-ed me._____ You need-ed me,_____ You need-ed me._____

TEDDY BEAR

Words & Music by DALE ROYAL, BILLY JOE BURNETTE, RED SOVINE & TOMMY HILL

Moderately Slow

RECITATION

I was on the outskirts of a little southern town; trying to reach
my destination before the sun went down...The CB was blaring away on
channel 19...when there came a little boy's voice on the radio line...
He said: "Breaker 19!...Is anyone there? Come on back, truckers...and
talk to Teddy Bear!"...I keyed the mike and said: "You got it, Teddy Bear!"
And a little boy's voice came back on the air..."'Preciate the break,...
Who we got on that end?"...
I told him my handle and he began:...

"I'm not supposed to bother you fellows out there...Mom says you're busy and for me to stay off the air...But you see, I get lonely and it helps to talk... 'cause that's all I can do...I'm crippled,...I can't walk!!!"

I came back and told him to fire up that mike...and I'd talk to him as long as he liked... "This was my dad's radio" the little boy said..."But I guess it's mine and mom's now, 'cause my dad's dead!"

"He had a wreck about a month ago...He was trying to get home in a blinding snow...Mom has to work now, to make ends meet...and I'm not much help with my two crippled feet!"

"She says not to worry...that we'll make it alright...But I hear her crying sometimes late at night...There's just one thing I want more than anything to see..Aw, I know you guys are too busy to bother with me!"

"But my dad used to take me for rides when he was home...but that's all over now, since my daddy's gone..." ...Not one breaker came on the old CB as the little crippled boy talked with me...I tried to swallow a lump that wouldn't stay down...as I thought about my boy back in Greenville Town.

"Dad was going to take mom and me with him later on this year...I remember him saying: 'Someday this old truck will be yours, Teddy Bear!'...But I know now I will never get to ride an 18 wheeler again ..but this old bas will keep me in touch with all my trucker friends!"

"Teddy Bear's gonna back on out now and leave you alone 'cause it's about time for mom to come home...Give me a shout when you're passing through...and I'll surely be happy to come back to you!"

I came back and said: "Before you go, 10 - 10...what's your home 20, little CB friend?"...He gave me his address and I didn't once hesitate...this hot load of freight would just have to wait!

I turned that truck around on a dime and headed for Jackson Street, 229... I round the corner and got one heck of a shock...18 wheelers were lined up for three city blocks!

Every driver for miles around had caught Teddy Bear's call...and that little crippled boy was having a ball...For as fast as one driver would carry him in, another would carry him to his truck and take off again.

Well, you better believe I took my turn riding Teddy Bear...and then carried him back in and put him down on his chair...And if I never live to see happiness again...I saw it that day in the face of that little man.

We took up a collection for him before his mama got home...Each driver said goodbye and then they were gone...He shook my hand with his mile-long grin and said: "So long, trucker...I'll catch you again!"

I hit the Interstate with tears in my eyes...I turned on the radio and got another surprise..."Breaker 19!" Came the voice on the air..."Just one word of thanks from Mama Teddy Bear!"

"We wish each and every one a special prayer for you...you made a little crippled boy's dream come true...I'll sign off now, before I start to cry... May God ride with you...10-4...and goodbye!"

STAND BY YOUR MAN

Words & Music by TAMMY WYNETTE & BILLY SHERRILL

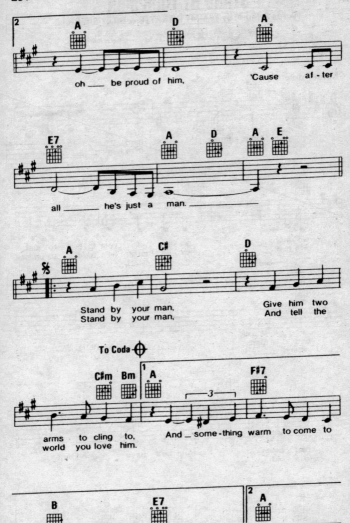

oh — be proud of him, 'Cause af-ter

all — he's just a man. —

Stand by your man,
Stand by your man,

Give him two
And tell the

To Coda ⊕

arms to cling to,
world you love him.

And — some-thing warm to come to

when nights are cold and lone-ly. Keep giv-ing

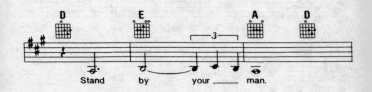

OLD DOGS, CHILDREN AND WATERMELON WINE

Words & Music by TOM T. HALL

Moderately

1. How old do you think I am, he said.

I said, well I did-n't know.

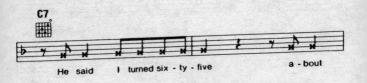

He said I turned six-ty-five   a-bout

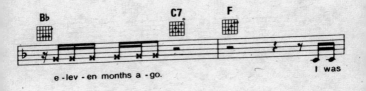

e-lev-en months a-go.   I was

sit-tin'   in Mi-am-i,____ pour-in' blend-ed whis-key

Gm / Bb / F

down ___ When this old grey - black gen - tle - man

C7 / F

was clean - in' up the lounge. 2. There

F7 / Bb

was - n't an - y - one a - round 'cept this old man __ and

Gm / C7

me. The guy __ who ran the bar was watch - in'

Bb / C7 / F

Iron - sides on T. V., Un - in - vit - ed

F7 / Bb

he sat down and o - pened ___ up his

mind ___ On old ___ dogs and chil-dren

and wa-ter-mel-on wine.

3. Ever had a drink of watermelon wine? He asked.
   He told me all about it though I didn't answer back.
   Ain't but three things in this world that's worth a solitary dime,
   But Old Dogs—Children And Watermelon Wine.

4. He said women think about theyselves when menfolk ain't around,
   And friends are hard to find when they discover that you down.
   He said I tried it all when I was young and in my natural prime;
   Now it's Old Dogs—Children And Watermelon Wine.

5. Old dogs care about you even when you make mistakes.
   God bless little children while they're still too young to hate.
   When he moved away, I found my pen and copied down that line
   'Bout old dogs and children and watermelon wine.

6. I had to catch a plane up to Atlanta that next day,
   As I left for my room I saw him pickin' up my change.
   That night I dreamed in peaceful sleep of shady summertime
   Of old dogs and children and watermelon wine.

SWINGIN'

Words & Music by JOHN DAVID ANDERSON & LIONEL A. DELMORE

With a strong beat

There's _____ a lit-tle girl

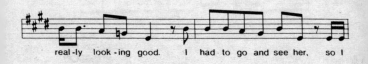

in our neigh-bor-hood. Her name is Char-lotte John-son, and she's

real-ly look-ing good. I had to go and see her, so I

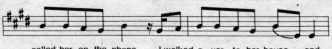

called her on the phone. I walked o-ver to her house,__ and

this was go-in' on: Her love down to my toes. And we was

CHORUS

swing - in', _____   (swing - in';)   yes, we was

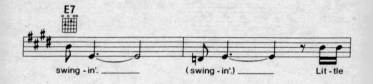

swing - in'. _____   (swing - in'.) _____   Lit - tle

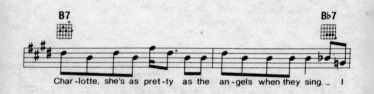

Char - lotte, she's as pret - ty   as the   an - gels when they sing. _   I

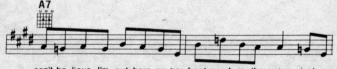

can't be - lieve I'm out here on her front porch in the swing,   just a

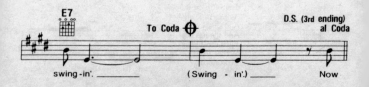

swing - in'. _____   (Swing - in'.) _____   Now

To Coda ⊕

D.S. (3rd ending)
al Coda

CODA

Lit-tle Char-lotte, she's as pret-ty as the

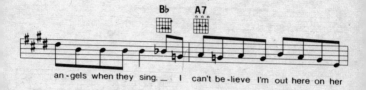

an-gels when they sing. __ I can't be-lieve I'm out here on her

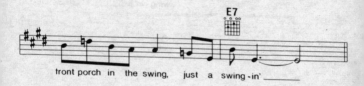

front porch in the swing, just a swing-in' _____

Repeat and Fade

(swing-in'. _____ swing-in'.) _____

Verse 2.
Her brother was on the sofa
Eatin' chocolate pie.
Her mama was in the kitchen
Cuttin' chicken up to fry.
Her daddy was in the backyard
Rollin' up a garden hose.
I was on the porch with Charlotte
Feelin' love down to my toes,
And we was swingin'.
(To Chorus)

Verse 3.
Now Charlotte, she's a darlin';
She's the apple of my eye.
When I'm on the swing with her
It makes me almost high.
And Charlotte is my lover.
And she has been since the spring.
I just can't believe it started
On her front porch in the swing.
(To Chorus)

HE STOPPED LOVING HER TODAY

Words & Music by BOBBY BRADDOCK & CURLY PUTMAN

He said, "I'll love you 'til I die",
He kept some let - ters by his bed,

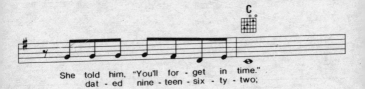

She told him, "You'll for - get in time."
dat - ed nine - teen - six - ty - two;

As the years went slow - ly by,
He had un - der - lined in red

she still preyed up - on his mind;
ev - ery sin - gle "I love you";

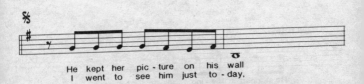

He kept her pic - ture on his wall
I went to see him just to - day,

and went half-cra-zy now and then;
but I did-n't see no tears;

But he still loved her through it all.
All dressed up to go a-way;

1

hop-ing she'd come back a-gain.

2,3

First time I'd seen him smile in years.

CHORUS

He stopped lov-ing her to-day;

They placed a wreath up - on his door; _____

And soon they'll car - ry him a - way; _____

To Coda

He stopped lov - ing her to - day. _____

D.S. (3rd ending)
al Coda

CODA

(Recite)

3. She came to see him one last time
   We all wondered if she would
   And it kept running through my mind
   This time he's over her for good. (REPEAT CHORUS)

FACTS

- More than 800,000 people go to the Grand Ole Opry show each year.
- Over 2 million visitors walk through the Country Music Hall of Fame each year.
- Nashville studios are responsible for one out of every two records produced today.
- In dollars, Nashville's music industry makes well over two hundred million a year.
- TEX RITTER became the first living person to be elected to Nashville's Country Music Hall of Fame in 1964.
- The Carter family was the first group admitted into the Country Music Hall of Fame in 1970. Known as the "First Family of Country Music."
- Acuff-Rose Publishing was Nashville's first exclusively country music publishing company and was co-founded in 1943.
- The first country music jamboree show was the "National Barn Dance" on WLS Chicago, which began April 19, 1924, by GEORGE D. HAY. Hay was the one who also started the Grand Ole Opry.

- The first Opry show was broadcast over WSM on November 28, 1925, and is considered to be the oldest show on radio.
- 1963 is the only year since the beginning of the Country Music Hall of Fame that no one was inducted into the Hall of Fame.
- To be selected as a Hall of Fame member, each year a committee of 100 members of CMA submit names. A name must receive 75% of the votes or 750 mentions on the list.
- Country record sales have always been consistent and steady . . . even during the Depression.
- Country records generally enjoy longer commercial life. For example, WLS Radio's hillbilly star BRADLEY KINCAID's "Fatal Wedding" was sold through the Sears & Roebuck catalog from 1928 to 1940.
- ERNEST TUBB was the first person to use electric guitars on country records.
- JIMMY TARLTON is reputed as being the first to use the steel guitar on a hillbilly record. His best-known releases were "Columbus Stockade Blues" and "Birmingham Jail."
- TEX WILLIAMS' "Smoke, Smoke, Smoke" gave Capitol Records their first million-seller.

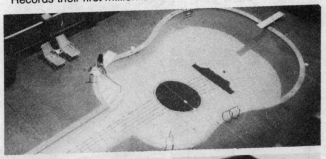

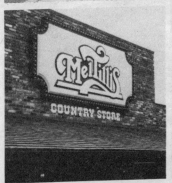

- The first film to use a singing cowboy was "Songs Of The Saddle" in 1930 with KEN MAYNARD.
- A black man named "Teetot" gave HANK WILLIAMS his first and only music lesson.
- Black railroad laborers taught JIMMIE RODGERS the banjo and guitar and many of their songs.
- DeFORD BAILEY was the first Negro to appear on the Opry and was famous for his harmonica playing.
- There is no Statler in the STATLER BROTHERS group today, and there never was.
- Harold Jenkins is still one of country music's biggest stars and consistently has hits under the name of CONWAY TWITTY.
- UNCLE DAVE MACON was billed and introduced as "The Dixie Dewdrop."
- ROY ACUFF is considered the "King of Country Music."
- KITTY WELLS is considered the "Queen of Country Music."
- BILL MONROE is considered the "Father of Bluegrass."
- ROY ROGERS is considered the "King of the Cowboys."
- BOB WILLS is considered the "King of Western Swing."

AUTHORS' AND
COMPOSERS' CREDITS

ALL I HAVE TO DO IS DREAM Boudleaux Bryant • **ALMOST PERSUADED** Glenn Sutton, Billy Sherrill • **AMANDA** Bob McDill • **(Hey, Won't You Play) ANOTHER SOMEBODY DONE SOMEBODY WRONG SONG** Larry Butler, Chips Moman • **ANY TIME** Herbert Happy Lawson • **ARE YOU LONESOME TONIGHT?** Lou Handman, Roy Turk • **BETTER HOMES AND GARDENS** Bobby Russell • **BLUE SUEDE SHOES** Carl Perkins • **A BOY NAMED SUE** Shel Silverstein • **A BROKEN HEARTED ME** Randy Goodrum • **BUSTED** Harlan Howard • **BYE BYE, LOVE** Boudleaux Bryant • **CHUG-A-LUG** Roger Miller • **COLD, COLD HEART** Hank Williams • **COUNTRY BUMPKIN** Don Wayne • **COUNTRY SUNSHINE** Billy Davis, Dottie West • **CRAZY** Willie Nelson • **CRAZY ARMS** Ralph Mooney, Charles Seals • **CRYING MY HEART OUT OVER YOU** Louise Certain, Marijohn Wilkin, Gladys Stacey, Carl Butler • **CRYSTAL CHANDELIERS** Ted Harris • **DADDY SANG BASS** Carl Perkins • **DANG ME** Roger Miller • **DETOUR** Paul Westmoreland • **DON'T BE CRUEL (To A Heart That's True)** Elvis Presley, Otis Blackwell • **DON'T TAKE YOUR GUNS TO TOWN** Johnny Cash • **DREAM ON LITTLE DREAMER** Fred Burch, Jan Crutchfield • **FADED LOVE** John Wills, Bob Wills • **FIVE FEET HIGH AND RISING** Johnny Cash • **FLOWERS ON THE WALL** Lewis Dewitt • **FOLSOM PRISON BLUES** Johnny Cash • **FUNNY HOW TIME SLIPS AWAY** Willie Nelson • **GONE** Smokey Rogers • **GOOD OLE BOYS LIKE ME** • Bob McDill • **GREEN GREEN GRASS OF HOME** Curly Putman • **THE HAPPIEST GIRL IN THE WHOLE U.S.A.** Donna Fargo • **HARPER VALLEY P.T.A.** Tom T. Hall • **HAVE I TOLD YOU LATELY THAT I LOVE YOU** Scott Wiseman • **HE STOPPED LOVING HER TODAY** Bobby Braddock • **HEARTACHES BY THE NUMBER** Harlan Howard • **HEARTBREAK HOTEL** Tommy Durden, Mae Boren Axton, Elvis Presley • **HELLO MARY LOU (Goodbye Heart)** Gene Pitney • **HELLO WALLS** Willie Nelson • **HEY, GOOD LOOKIN'** Hank Williams • **HONEY** Bobby Russell • **I AIN'T NEVER** Mel Tillis, Webb Pierce • **I FALL TO PIECES** Harlan Howard, Hank Cochran • **I LOVE** Tom T. Hall • **I SAW THE LIGHT** Hank Williams • **I WALK THE LINE** Johnny Cash • **I'M SO LONESOME I COULD CRY** Hank Williams • **I'M SORRY** Ronnie Self, Dub Albritton • **IF DRINKIN' DON'T KILL ME, HER MEMORY WILL** Harlan Sanders, Rick Beresford • **IT TURNS ME INSIDE OUT** Jan Crutchfield • **IT'S NOW OR NEVER** Wally Gold, Aaron Schroeder • **JAMBALAYA (On The Bayou)** Hank Williams •

JUST A LITTLE LOVIN' (Will Go A Long Way) Zeke Clements, Eddy Arnold • **KAW-LIGA** Hank Williams, Fred Rose • **KING OF THE ROAD** Roger Miller • **KISS AN ANGEL GOOD MORNIN'** Ben Peters • **LITTLE GREEN APPLES** Bobby Russell • **THE LONG BLACK VEIL** Danny Dill, Marijohn Wilkin • **LORD MR. FORD** Dick Feller • **LOVE ME TENDER** Vera Matson, Elvis Presley • **MAKE THE WORLD GO AWAY** Hank Cochran • **MY HEROES HAVE ALWAYS BEEN COW-BOYS** Sharon Vaughn • **NOBODY LIKES SAD SONGS** Wayland Holyfield, Bob McDill • **OLD DOGS, CHILDREN AND WATERMELON WINE** Tom T. Hall • **PAPER MANSIONS** Ted Harris • **PLEASE HELP ME, I'M FALLING (In Love With You)** Don Robertson, Hal Blair • **RAINING IN MY HEART** Boudleaux Bryant, Felice Bryant • **(Remember Me) I'M THE ONE WHO LOVES YOU** Stuart Hamblen • **ROCKY TOP** Boudleaux Bryant, Felice Bryant • **ROOM FULL OF ROSES** Tim Spencer • **RUBY, DON'T TAKE YOUR LOVE TO TOWN** Mel Tillis • **RUN-NING BEAR** J.P. Richardson • **SATIN SHEETS** John E. Volinkaty • **SAVE THE LAST DANCE FOR ME** Doc Pomus, Mort Shuman • **SAVE YOUR HEART FOR ME** Bob McDill • **SHUTTERS AND BOARDS** Audie Murphy, Scott Turner • **SIXTEEN TONS** Merle Travis • **SKIP A ROPE** Jack Moran, Glenn D. Tubb • **SOMEBODY'S KNOCKIN'** Ed Penney, Jerry Gillespie • **SOMEDAY MY DAY WILL COME** Earl Montgomery, Christopher C. Ryder, V.L. Haywood • **SOMEONE TO GIVE MY LOVE TO** Jerry Foster, Bill Rice • **STAND BY YOUR MAN** Tammy Wynette, Billy Sherrill • **SWINGIN'** John David Anderson, Lionel A. Delmore • **TALK ABOUT THE GOOD TIMES** Jerry Reed Hubbard • **TEDDY BEAR** Red Sovine, Dale Royal, Billy Joe Burnette, Tommy Hill • **THANK GOD AND GREYHOUND** Ed Nix, Larry Kingston • **A THING CALLED LOVE** Jerry Reed Hubbard • **U.S. MALE** Jerry Reed Hubbard • **WAKE UP, LITTLE SUSIE** Felice Bryant, Boudleaux Bryant • **WATERLOO** John Loudermilk, Marijohn Wilkin • **WHEN TWO WORLDS COLLIDE** Roger Miller, Bill Anderson • **WHEN YOU'RE HOT, YOU'RE HOT** Jerry Reed Hubbard • **Y'ALL COME BACK SALOON** Sharon Vaughn • **YESTERDAY, WHEN I WAS YOUNG (Hier Encore)** Herbert Kretzmer, Charles Aznavour • **YOU NEEDED ME** Randy Goodrum • **YOU'RE THE BEST BREAK THIS OLD HEART EVER HAD** Randy Hatch, Wayland Holyfield • **YOUR CHEATIN' HEART** Hank Williams

NASHVILLE MUSIC PUBLISHERS

Acuff-Rose Music
Ahab Music
Almo Irving Music
American Cowboy Music
ATV Music
Beechwood Music
Ben Speer Music
The Benson Company, Inc.
Blackwood Music
Blendingwell Music
Roger Bowling Music
Briarpatch Music
Buckhorn Music
Buzz Cason Publications
Canaanland Music
CBS Songs
Cedarwood Music
    Publishing Co., Inc.
Chappel & Company
Chess Music
Jerry Chestnut Music
Coal Miners Music
Colgems Music Corp.
Combine Music Group
Con Brio Music
Cristy Lane Music
Cross Keys Pub. Co.
DebDave Music
Dick James Music Inc.
Don Gant Music
Drake Music Group
Ernest Tubb Music
Famous Music
    Publishing Co.
Faron Young Music
Fifty Grand Music
First Lady's Songs
Floyd Cramer Music
Al Gallico Music
Hallnote Music Co.

Hall-Clement Publishing Co.
John Hartford Music
Harbot Music
House Of Bryant Music
House Of Cash Music
House Of Gold Music
Intersong Music
Jack Music
Jerry Foster Music
Kelso Herston Music
Mastercraft Music
Maypop Music
MCA Music
OAS Music Group
Old Friends Music
Tommy Overstreet
    Enterprises
Pannin' Gold
    Music Publishers
Paragon Publishing Group
Peer-Southern Organization
Ed Penney Productions
Picalic Music
Porter Music Company
Pride Music Group
Prime Time Music
Jeanne Pruett Music Inc.
Jim Reeves Enterprises
Resaca Music
Bill Rice Productions Inc.
Sawgrass Music
Screen Gems-EMI Music
Shade Tree Music
Shelby Singleton Music
Show Biz Music
Silverline-Goldline Music
Singletree Music
Snowfox Music
Southern Writers Group
Stamps Quartet Music Co.

Stick Horse Music Corp.
Stuckey Publishing Co.
Sure Fire Music Co., Inc.
Sylvia's Mother's Music Inc.
Tom Collins Music
Tree Publishing Co.
Triune Music
Twitty Bird Music

United Artist
  Music Publishing Co.
Vector Music
Warner Bros. Music
Welbeck Music Corp.
Welk Music Group
Window Music
  Publishing Co.
Word Record & Music Group

NASHVILLE
RECORD COMPANIES
AND RECORDING STUDIOS

Audio Media Recorders
Beaverwood
  Recording Studio
Bullet Recording
Capitol Records Inc.
The Cassette Connection
CBS Records
Cedarwood Sound Studio
Celebration Productions
Chips Moman's
  Recording Studio
Creative Workshop Inc.
Doc's Place
  Recording Studio
Elektra
Emerald Sound Studio Inc.
Fireside
  Recording Studio Inc.
Glaser Sound Studios Inc.
Gusto Recording Studios
Hilltop Recording Studio Inc.
LSI Recording
Liberty Records
MCA Records
Music City Music Hall
The Music Mill
Oak Valley Sound
  Recording Studio

Pete's Place
  Recording Studio
Pollyfox Recording Studio
Quadrafonic Sound Studio
RCA Records
Randy's Roost
The Reflections
Scruggs Sound Studio
Shock House
The Shook Shack
Skylite-Sing Recording Co.
Sound Emporium
  Recording Studio
Sound Lab
Sound Stage Studio
Soundshop
  Recording Studio, Inc.
Stargem Production Studio
Studio By The Pond
Superior Sound Studios
Treasure Isle Recorders
U.S. Recording Studio
Vasser Studio
Warner Bros. Records
Wild Tracks
  Recording Studio
Woodland Sound Studios
Young'un Sound Inc.

ARTISTS WHO HAVE RECORDED IN NASHVILLE

Roy Acuff • Alabama • Rex Allen • Rex Allen Jr. • Allman Brothers Band • Amazing Rhythm Aces • Ed Ames • Bill Anderson • John Anderson • Lynn Anderson • Julie Andrews • Paul Anka • Louis Armstrong • Eddy Arnold • Asleep At The Wheel • Chet Atkins • Gene Autry • Hoyt Axton • Joan Baez • Judy Bailey • Razzy Bailey • Bandana • Moe Bandy • Bobby Bare • Barefoot Jerry • Bellamy Brothers • Brook Benton • Debby Boone • Pat Boone • Boy's Band • Owen Bradley • Terry Bradshaw • Bonnie Bramlett • Kippi Brannon • James Brown • Jim Ed Brown • The Browns • Ed Bruce • Anita Bryant • Jimmy Buffett • George Burns • Burrito Brothers • The Byrds • Shirley Caesar • Thomas Cain • Calamity Jane • David Cassidy • J.J. Cale • Glen Campbell • Kim Carnes • Vicki Carr • Martha Carson • The Carter Family • Johnny Cash • Rosanne Cash • Carol Channing • Gary Chapman • Ray Charles • Roy Clark • Vassar Clements • Patsy Cline • Rosemary Clooney • Joe Cocker • David Allen Coe • Jessi Colter • Perry Como • John Conlee • Earl Thomas Conley • Elvis Costello • Gene Cotton • Billy "Crash" Craddock • Floyd Cramer • The Crescendos • Rodney Crowell • The Crusaders • The Commodores • Vic Damone • Dallas Cowboys Cheerleaders • Charlie Daniels Band • Lacy J. Dalton • Gail Davies • Mac Davis • Skeeter Davis • Jimmy Dean • John Denver • Little Jimmy Dickens • Dillard & Boyce • Dean Dillon • Fats Domino • Donovan • Ronnie Dove • Big Al Downing • Pete Drake • Dr. Hook • Roy Drusky • Bob Dylan • Clint Eastwood • Duane Eddy • Barbara Eden • England Dan & John Ford Coley • Everly Brothers • Exile • Barbara Fairchild • Donna Fargo • Dick Feller • Narvel Felts • Freddie Fender • Firefall • Flatt & Scruggs • Dan Fogelberg • Red Foley • Tennessee Ernie Ford • Pete Fountain • Connie Francis • Dallas Frazier • Janie Fricke • David Frizzell • Lefty Frizzell • Art Garfunkel • James Garner • Larry Gatlin • Crystal Gayle • The Gentrys • Terri Gibbs • Don Gibson • Mickey Gilley • Tompall & The Glaser Brothers • George Gobel • Bobby Goldsboro • Leslie Gore • Edie Gorme • Frank Gorshin • Vern Gosdin • Billy Grammer • Grand Funk Railroad • Amy Grant • Dobie Gray • Jack Greene • Lorne Greene • Lee Greenwood • Grinderswitch • Arlo Guthrie • Merle Haggard • Tom T. Hall • George Hamilton IV • Emmylou Harris • John Hartford • Hawkshaw Hawkins • Goldie Hawn • Levon Helm • Jimi Hendrix • Woody Herman • Al Hirt • Don Ho • Buddy Holly • Homer & Jethro • Johnny Horton • David Houston • Engelbert Humperdinck • Ferlin Husky • Burl Ives • Stonewall Jackson • Wanda Jackson • The James Gang • Sonny James • Waylon Jennings • Billy Joel • Michael Johnson • Bobby Jones • George Jones • Grandpa Jones • Jack Jones • Tom Jones • The Jordanaires • Kansas • KC & The Sunshine Band • The Kendalls • Anita Kerr • Doug Kershaw • Pee Wee King • Gladys Knight & The Pips • Al Kooper • Kris Kristofferson • Don King •

B.B. King • Jayne Kennedy • Frankie Laine • McGuffey Lane • Steve Lawrence • Brenda Lee • Dickey Lee • Johnny Lee • Jerry Lee Lewis • Gordon Lightfoot • Little Richard • Little River Band • Lobo • Dave Loggins • Loggins & Messina • Claudine Longet • Bob Luman • Loretta Lynn • Barbara Mandrell • Louise Mandrell • Chuck Mangione • Manhattan Transfer • Ann-Margret • Marshall Tucker Band • Dean Martin • C.W. McCall • Paul McCartney • Delbert McClinton • Mel McDaniel • Ronnie McDowell • Don McLean • Bill Medley • Melanie • Jody Miller • Roger Miller • Steve Miller • Ronnie Milsap • Robert Mitchum • The Monkees • Bill Monroe • Melba Montgomery • Michael Murphy • Anne Murray • Ricky Nelson • Tracy Nelson • Willie Nelson • The Newbeats • Micky Newbury • Jimmy C. Newman • Olivia Newton-John • Wayne Newton • Nitty Gritty Dirt Band • Oak Ridge Boys • Kenny O'Dell • Roy Orbison • Marie Osmond • Buck Owens • Ozark Mountain Daredevils • Tony Orlando • Patti Page • Dolly Parton • Les Paul • Minnie Pearl • Carl Perkins • Webb Pierce • Ray Pillow • Sandy Posey • Pozo-Seco Singers • Elvis Presley • Ray Price • Charley Pride • John Prine • Pure Prairie League • Johnny Paycheck • Eddie Rabbitt • Boots Randolph • Lou Rawls • Eddy Raven • Helen Reddy • Jerry Reed • Del Reeves • Jim Reeves • R.E.O. Speedwagon • Charlie Rich • Riders In The Sky • Jeannie C. Riley • Tex Ritter • Johnny Rivers • Marty Robbins • Johnny Rodriguez • Tommy Roe • Kenny Rogers • Roy Rogers • Linda Ronstadt • Billy Joe Royal • Bobby Russell • Leon Russell • S. Sgt. Berry Sadler • Buffy Saint-Marie • Sam & Dave • John Schneider • Jack Scott • Earl Scruggs • Seals & Croft • Pete Seeger • Jeannie Seely • Del Shannon • Jean Shepard • T.G. Sheppard • Dinah Shore • Simon & Garfunkel • Joe Simon • Frank Sinatra • Frank Sinatra Jr. • Nancy Sinatra • Ricky Skaggs • Sister Sledge • Cal Smith • Sammi Smith • Hank Snow • Sons Of The Pioneers • Joe South • Sissy Spacek • Billy Jo Spears • Jim Stafford • Joe Stampley • Ringo Starr • The Statler Brothers • Ray Stevens • Gary Stewart • George Strait • Joe Sun • Billy Swan • Joe Tex • B.J. Thomas • Hank Thompson • Mel Tillis • Pam Tillis • Johnny Tillotson • Lily Tomlin • Merle Travis • Tanya Tucker • Twiggy • Conway Twitty • Bobby Vinton • The Vogues • Porter Wagoner • Billy Walker • Jerry Jeff Walker • Joe Walsh • Steve Wariner • Jennifer Warnes • Dionne Warwick • Doc Watson • Kitty Wells • Dottie West • Shelly West • Billy Ed Wheeler • The Whites • Tony Joe White • Slim Whitman • Roger Whittaker • Andy Williams • Don Williams • Hank Williams • Hank Williams Jr. • Paul Williams • Bob Wills • Edgar Winter • Johnny Winter • Del Wood • Tammy Wynette • Faron Young • Neil Young

HISTORY OF THE COUNTRY MUSIC ASSOCIATION

For the past 25 years, the Country Music Association has steadily and industriously promoted the growth and understanding of country music around the nation and around the world.

Since its founding in 1958, CMA's membership has grown from the original 200 to more than 7,000 Country Music professionals. It was the first trade organization ever formed to promote a type of music. The tremendous impact of the Association's efforts can be measured today, during its 25th anniversary year, by the popularity of Country Music throughout the world. Country music is truly a major sociological as well as musical influence, whose effects are manifest in every facet of society.

The CMA was "country when country wasn't cool." Believing in the viability of country music, CMA deliberately pushed on, finding innovative ways to spread the word. Highlights of the Association's many contributions to the industry include:

- **THE CMA AWARDS** — Prestigious accolade to top country acts voted upon by CMA members, founded in 1967. The CMA Awards Show has been on national television since 1968.
- **FAN FAIR** — One of the world's biggest country music celebrations! Co-sponsored with the Grand Ole Opry, the annual International Country Music Fan Fair attracts thousands of fans who come from throughout the world to meet their favorite stars, and to see exhibits and shows.
- **CLOSE-UP MAGAZINE** — Monthly publication giving pertinent information and industry trends for all members.
- **INTERNATIONAL OFFICE** — The growth of the country music industry necessitated the opening of a branch office in London.
- **DJ AWARDS** — Given each year to the top country music disc jockeys in small, medium and large market areas.
- **TALENT BUYERS SEMINAR** — To promote the use of country acts in fairs, auditoriums, parks, theaters and such.

- **INFORMATION SOURCE** — The CMA is recognized throughout the music industry and beyond as the definitive source on the growth of country music . . . past and future.
- **COUNTRY MUSIC HALL OF FAME** — Honoring country music greats, and building the Hall Of Fame Museum.
- **LEGISLATIVE SUPPORT** — To aid bills to benefit the industry.

Through the untiring efforts of the membership of the Country Music Association, the industry is experiencing phenomenal growth and influence around the world today. This membership continues to make country music the shining star in today's entertainment industry.

CMA AWARD WINNERS

ENTERTAINER OF THE YEAR:

1967 — Eddy Arnold
1968 — Glen Campbell
1969 — Johnny Cash
1970 — Merle Haggard
1971 — Charley Pride
1972 — Loretta Lynn
1973 — Roy Clark
1974 — Charlie Rich
1975 — John Denver
1976 — Mel Tillis
1977 — Ronnie Milsap
1978 — Dolly Parton
1979 — Willie Nelson
1980 — Barbara Mandrell
1981 — Barbara Mandrell
1982 — Alabama
1983 — Alabama

SONG OF THE YEAR:

1967 — "There Goes My Everything" — Dallas Frazier
1968 — "Honey" — Bobby Russell
1969 — "Carroll County Accident" — Bob Ferguson
1970 — "Sunday Morning Coming Down" — Kris Kristofferson
1971 — "Easy Loving" — Freddie Hart
1972 — "Easy Loving" — Freddie Hart
1973 — "Behind Closed Doors" — Kenny O'Dell
1974 — "Country Bumpkin" — Don Wayne
1975 — "Back Home Again" — John Denver
1976 — "Rhinestone Cowboy" — Larry Weiss
1977 — "Lucille" — Roger Bowling & Hal Bynum
1978 — "Don't It Make My Brown Eyes Blue" — Richard Leigh
1979 — "The Gambler" — Don Schlitz — Writer's Night Music
1980 — "He Stopped Loving Her Today" — Bobby Braddock & Curly Putman — Tree Publications
1981 — "He Stopped Loving Her Today" — Bobby Braddock & Curly Putman — Tree Publications
1982 & 1983 — "Always On My Mind" — Johnny Christopher, Wayne Thompson, Mark James — Screen Gems, EMI Music, Rose Bridge Music

COUNTRY MUSIC
HALL OF FAME NOMINEES

Election to the Country Music Hall of Fame is the crowning achievement in the career of a member of the country music industry. The Hall of Fame was founded in 1961 by the Country Music Association and currently has 35 members.

Hall of Fame inductees are selected each year by an anonymous panel of 200 electors, each of whom has actively participated in the music business for at least fifteen years and has made a significant contribution to the industry. These electors vote by secret ballot, the results of which are tallied by the national accounting firm of Deloitte Haskins & Sells. Winners are traditionally announced on the CMA Awards Show in October. The Hall of Fame election, itself, is conducted by the Country Music Association.

COUNTRY MUSIC HALL OF FAME INDUCTEES

	Year Elected
Jimmie Rodgers	1961
Fred Rose	1961
Hank Williams	1961
Roy Acuff	1962
Tex Ritter	1964
Ernest Tubb	1965
Eddy Arnold	1966
James R. Denny	1966
George D. Hay	1966
Uncle Dave Macon	1966
Red Foley	1967
J.L. (Joe) Frank	1967
Jim Reeves	1967
Stephen H. Sholes	1967
Bob Wills	1968
Gene Autry	1969
Bill Monroe	1969
Original Carter Family:	
A.P. Carter	1970
Maybelle Carter	1970
Sara Carter	1970
Arthur Edward Satherley	1971
Jimmie H. Davis	1972
Chet Atkins	1973
Patsy Cline	1973

	Year Elected
Owen Bradley	1974
Frank "Pee Wee" King	1974
Minnie Pearl	1975
Paul Cohen	1976
Kitty Wells	1976
Merle Travis	1977
Grandpa Jones	1978
Hank Snow	1979
Hubert Long	1979
Johnny Cash	1980
Connie B. Gay	1980
Original Sons Of The Pioneers:	
Hugh Farr	1980
Karl Farr	1980
Bob Nolan	1980
Lloyd Perryman	1980
Roy Rogers	1980
Tim Spencer	1980
Vernon Dalhart	1981
Grant Turner	1981
Lefty Frizzell	1982
Roy Horton	1982
Marty Robbins	1982
"Little" Jimmy Dickens	1983

PROFESSIONAL MUSIC ORGANIZATIONS AND ASSOCIATIONS

In the Nashville Area

American Society of Composers Authors and Publishers (ASCAP)
2 Music Square West
Nashville, TN 37203
615/244-3936

Country Music Association (CMA)
7 Music Circle North
Nashville, TN 37203
615/244-2840

Gospel Music Association (GMA)
38 Music Square West
Nashville, TN 37203
615/242-0303

Nashville Music Association (NMA)
P.O. Box 25309
Nashville, TN 37202
615/242-9662

Nashville Symphony Association
1805 West End Ave.
Nashville, TN 37203
615/329-3033

Nashville Area Chamber of Commerce
161 4th Ave. North
Nashville, TN 37219
615/259-3900

Broadcast Music, Inc. (BMI)
11 Music Square East
Nashville, TN 37203
615/259-3625

Country Music Foundation (CMF)
4 Music Square East
Nashville, TN 37203
615/256-1639

National Academy of Recording Arts and Sciences (NARAS)
7 Music Circle North
Nashville, TN 37203
615/255-8777

Nashville Songwriters Association, International (NSAI)
803 18th Ave. South
Nashville, TN 37203
615/321-5004

SESAC
11 Music Circle South
Nashville, TN 37203
615/244-1992

Tennessee Association of Broadcasters
4701 Trousdale Dr.
Nashville, TN 37204
615/331-4535

Belmont College
School of Business
Music Business
1900 Belcourt Avenue
Nashville, TN 37203

Middle Tennessee State University
Dept. of Mass Communications
Recording Industry Management
Murfreesboro, TN 37130

ADAGIO — 23 Union; 259-1234. Features a piano bar for entertainment. Placed in elegant surroundings of the Hyatt Regency Downtown.

ANDERSON'S CAJUN'S WHARF — 901 Cowan St.; 254-7711. Settled beside the Cumberland River, this restaurant/club offers some of the best Louisiana seafood cuisine in town. Cajun's also offers nightly entertainment featuring country, pop and rock. There's even a dance floor for those who love to dance.

BLUEBIRD CAFE — 4104 Hillsboro Rd.; 383-1461. Features live country, jazz and rock music nightly. The cafe specializes in entertainment by some of country music's noted songwriters and entertainers.

BLUEGRASS INN — Corner of Broadway and Lyle. Features bluegrass music every weekend performed by Hubert Davis and The Season Travelers.

BOGEY'S — 80 White Bridge Rd.; 352-2447. This restaurant/club specializes in bringing the best of Nashville's local talent to stage. From country to jazz to rock-n-roll and blues, Bogey's brings all forms of music to Nashville.

BOOTS RANDOLPH'S — 209 Printer's Alley; 256-5500. This club is in historic Printer's Alley and should be visited especially by fans of the "Yakety-Sax" man, Boots Randolph. Randolph and his saxophone perform six nights a week with music from the big band era.

THE CANNERY — 811 Palmer; 256-5310. A nightspot that presents country, western, bluegrass and rock music all at the same time. The three separate lounges at the Cannery allow for a variety of music and dancing to fit everyone's taste.

CANTRELLS — 1901 Broadway; 327-2356. For those who enjoy a little "punk" music or a "new wave" sound, Cantrells is the place to go. They also feature regular rock-n-roll, country and blues.

THE CAROUSEL DINNER CLUB — 220 Printer's Alley; 244-8391. Home of Ronnie Prophet. This club is set in famous Printer's Alley and has continuous entertainment.

CELLAR LOUNGE — 1907 West End Ave.; 321-5141. Located in the "cellar" of Baudo's Italian Restaurant, this piano bar provides entertainment by some of Nashville's finest songwriters and entertainers.

THE EMBERS SHOWCASE — 210 Printer's Alley; 254-6616. This showroom is located in Printer's Alley and presents outstanding entertainment. The famous comedy team of Eddie and Joe appear nightly.

FOUR GUYS HARMONY HOUSE — 407 Murfreesboro Rd.; 256-0188. This club provides great country music by Grand Ole Opry stars The Four Guys.

THE GOLDRUSH — 2205 Elliston Place; 327-2809. For some of the best Mexican food in town, this is the place to go. They also have entertainment every Friday and Saturday which spotlights some of Nashville's local talent.

THE NASHVILLE PALACE — 2400 McGavock Pike; 885-1540. Offers live music that is only *country*. Monday nights are especially well-known for being Opry Star Night, in which a member of the Grand Ole Opry performs.

THE STATION INN — 402 12th Ave. South; 255-3307. This club has all the best in bluegrass. The casual atmosphere has featured some of the most famous bluegrass artists around. They are especially popular for their Sunday Bluegrass Jam Night.

STOCKYARD RESTAURANT AND BULL PEN LOUNGE — 901 2nd Ave. North; 255-6464. This club is owned partly by Conway Twitty, T.G. Sheppard and the Gatlin Brothers, and is known as a place where "you can never tell who might pop in."

WESTERN ROOM — 210 4th Ave. North; 256-9339. Located in Printer's Alley, this club features some of Nashville's best country and western entertainers, and is one of the most popular clubs in the Alley.

WRANGLERS — 1204 Murfreesboro Rd.; 361-4440. The Wranglers has one of the most "sociable" happy hours and buffets in town. Also one of the best dance floors, especially if you're interested in the two-step.

RESTAURANTS IN THE NASHVILLE AREA

ANDERSON'S CAJUN'S WHARF — 901 Cowan St.; 254-7711. Creole cuisine and seafood are their specialty.

APPLEGATE'S LANDING — 3754 Nolensville Rd.; 832-3199. For family eating in a friendly atmosphere.

ARTHUR'S — The Mall at Green Hills; 383-8841. Mobil Four Star Award winner. Six-course dinners vary nightly.

BAUDO'S RESTAURANT — 1907 West End Ave.; 321-5141. Offers the very finest in Italian and American cuisine.

BOGEY'S — 80 White Bridge Rd.; 352-2447. Good food in a leisurely atmosphere with nightly entertainment.

BOOTS RANDOLPH'S — 209 Printer's Alley; 256-5500. This is a plush dinner club that is the home of "Mr. Sax," Boots Randolph.

BROADWAY BAKERY — 2005 Broadway; 327-9567. For elegant dining in an elegant atmosphere reminiscent of a French bakery.

BROWN'S DINER — 2102 Blair Blvd.; 269-5509. For a relaxed atmosphere and great down-home cooking. This is a favorite spot for locals.

THE CAPTAIN'S TABLE — Printer's Alley; 251-9535. A popular nightspot in Printer's Alley, steak and lobster are their specialties.

CASA GALLARDO — 24 White Bridge Rd.; 356-3165. Serves fine Mexican food.

CIRACO'S RESTAURANT — 212 21st Ave. South; 329-0036. Fine Italian cuisine. Ciraco's has a family dining area for a relaxed atmosphere and a Gourmet Dining Room for more elegant dining.

CLOSE QUARTERS — 913 20th Ave. South; 327-1115. Decorative, glass-enclosed dining room and outdoor patio area, serving authentic Mexican specialties.

CROWN COURT — **2025 Metrocenter Blvd., in the Maxwell House Hotel; 259-4343.** Elegant, skylighted restaurant that gives you a view of downtown. Mobil Travel Guide Four Star Award winner. Their continental cuisine features specialties like lamb and veal.

FAISON'S — **2000 Belcourt Ave.; 320-1555.** Faison's has a cozy, off-beat atmosphere set in an old house with jazz on stereo.

FOUR GUYS HARMONY HOUSE — **407 Murfreesboro Rd.; 256-0188.** Dining, dancing and entertainment by Grand Ole Opry stars The Four Guys.

FRIDAY'S — **2214 Elliston Place; 329-9575.** A weekend atmosphere — every day!

THE GERST HOUSE — **228 Woodland St.; 256-9760.** A place that serves authentic German cuisine.

HERMITAGE DINING ROOM — **231 6th Ave. North, in the Hermitage Hotel; 244-3121.** An atmosphere captured from decades gone by, located in the beautifully restored Hermitage Hotel. An elegant restaurant, winner of the Mobil Four Star Award for excellence.

HOUSTON'S RESTAURANT — **3000 West End Ave.; 269-3481.** From a popular happy hour to family dining, Houston's menu alone will keep you coming back.

HUGO'S GOURMET DINING — **623 Union St., in the Hyatt Regency Hotel; 259-1234.** Elegant decor that specializes in continental and Japanese cuisine.

HUNGRY FISHERMAN — **115 Cumberland Bend; 254-3541.** Seafood is the name of the game in this beautiful restaurant on an island in its own little lake.

HUNT ROOM — **4th and Union, in the Radisson Plaza Hotel; 244-8200.** Polished decor reflects hunt motif. Their specialty is dinners before and after Tennessee Performing Arts Center performances.

JIMMY KELLY'S — **217 Louise Ave.; 329-4349.** Excellent family eating. All entrées are accompanied by their FAMOUS corncakes.

JULIAN'S — **2412 West End Ave.; 327-2412.** Four Star Mobil Travel Guide Award. Julian's specialty is French cuisine.

KOBE STEAK HOUSE — **210 25th Ave. North; 327-9081.** Traditional Japanese dishes served with a flair for showmanship.

LOVELESS MOTEL AND RESTAURANT — **Highway 100; 646-9700.** For the best "down home" eating in Nashville. Especially noted for their homemade biscuits.

MARIO'S — **1915 West End Ave.; 327-3232.** A Four Star Restaurant by the Mobil Travel Guide. Mario's features cuisine in the Italian manner.

MARK'S 325 UNION — **325 Union St.; 242-7777.** This downtown pub is an ideal spot, especially before or after an attendance at the Tennessee Performing Arts Center.

MAUDE'S COURTYARD — **1911 Broadway; 320-0543.** A remodeled house with a glassed-in courtyard. A favorite hangout for music industry personnel.

MIKADO JAPANESE STEAK HOUSE — 410 Metroplex Dr.; 832-8300. Japanese specialties in an elegant atmosphere.

MY PLACE — 907 20th Ave. South; 329-9144. A relaxed atmosphere in a restored house with eating inside or outside on the patio.

NEW ORLEANS MANOR — 1400 Murfreesboro Rd.; 367-2777. All-you-can-eat seafood buffet in an elegant Southern manor house.

O'CHARLEY'S RESTAURANT — 402 21st Ave. South; 327-3773. Good food in an informal atmosphere.

OLD SPAGHETTI FACTORY — 160 2nd Ave. North; 254-9010. This was once a downtown warehouse, but has been transformed into a restaurant that specializes in spaghetti. An ideal place to take the family.

OLD HICKORY RESTAURANT — 2800 Opryland Dr., in the Opryland Hotel; 889-1000. Fine dining in elegant surroundings with cuisine and service in the finest tradition. A truly memorable dining experience.

101st AIRBORNE — 1360 Murfreesboro Rd.; 361-4212. This restaurant is reminiscent of World War II, with photographs of soldiers and total decor set to be an airbase.

THE PEDDLER STEAK HOUSE — 110 Lyle Ave.; 327-2325. Comfortable, candlelit atmosphere with steak as their specialty.

PEKING GARDEN RESTAURANT — 1923 Division; 327-2020. Oriental cuisine at its very finest.

QUARTER NOTE RESTAURANT — 913 20th Ave. South; 327-1115. Fine Mexican food at its best.

ROTIER'S RESTAURANT — 2413 Elliston Place; 327-9892. The best hamburgers, chili and steaks can be found in this "homey" restaurant. Another one of those places that usually only "hometowners" know about.

SAILMAKER RESTAURANT — 4243 Harding Rd.; 298-2645. Distinctive nautical decor, specializing in seafood.

SPATS RESTAURANT — 1601 21st Ave. South; 320-7130. Good eating in friendly surroundings and atmosphere of an earlier time when women carried frilly umbrellas and men wore spats.

SPINNAKERS RESTAURANT — 3808 Cleghorn Ave.; 298-5435. This restaurant offers good food and a good time.

STOCKYARD — 901 2nd Ave. North; 255-6464. This restaurant is located in the restored Union Stockyard downtown. The house specialty is steak cut from corn-fed beef.

TONY ROMA'S PLACE — 2212 Elliston Place; 329-1122. If ribs are what you want, then Tony Roma's is the place to go for the best ribs in town.

VILLA ROMANO — 2007 Terrace Place; 327-2185. Elegant, Italian Renaissance decor in a refurbished house. Northern Italian and continental cuisine are featured.

ATTRACTIONS IN AND AROUND THE NASHVILLE AREA

THE JIM REEVES MUSEUM — Located in historic Evergreen Mansion, the museum contains personal items of the late Jim Reeves. 1023 Joyce Lane; 226-2062. Hours: 9am-6pm, seven days a week

MUSIC VALLEY WAX MUSEUM — contains over 40 lifelike wax figures of favorite country stars. 2515 McGavock Pike; 883-3612. Hours: daily 9am-9pm, May 20 - Sept. 10; Mon. - Thurs. 9am-5pm, Sept. 11 - Oct.; Fri. and Sat. 9am-6pm; and daily 9am-5pm, Nov. - May 19

OPRYLAND, U.S.A. — a 120-acre showpark which contains shows, rides, restaurants and specialty shops which are all centered around the theme of "American Music." Opryland Dr.; 889-6611. Hours: daily 10am-10pm, May 30 - Sept. 5; 10am-5pm, March 26 - May 29 and Sept. 10 - Oct. 30

GRAND OLE OPRY — Internationally famed Opry shows are performed each Friday and Saturday nights. 2804 Opryland Dr.; 889-3060. Hours: 6:30pm and 9:30pm

TENNESSEE STATE MUSEUM — in the James K. Polk Building, features history of Tennessee. 505 Deaderick; 741-2692. Hours: 10am-5pm, Mon. - Fri.; 1pm-5pm, Sun.

TENNESSEE PERFORMING ARTS CENTER — offers Broadway shows, major orchestras, ballet and other spectacular events. 505 Deaderick St.; 741-2787. Hours: 9am-6pm, Mon. - Fri.

FORT NASHBOROUGH — a reproduction of the original stockade that protected Nashville and its early settlers in 1780. 170 1st Ave. North; 255-8192. Hours: 9am-4pm, Tues. - Sun.

RYMAN AUDITORIUM — home of the Grand Ole Opry from 1943 until March 16, 1974. 116 5th Ave. North; 749-1445. Hours: daily 8:30am-4:30pm

PARTHENON — The world's only replica of the Athenian temple is located in Nashville's Centennial Park. Centennial Park; 259-6358. Hours: 9am-4:30pm, Tues. - Sat.; 1pm-4:30pm, Sun.

THE CAR COLLECTOR'S HALL OF FAME — features cars of country music stars plus rare antique automobiles. 1534 Demonbreun; 244-2527. Hours: daily 8am-8pm, June - Aug.; daily 8:30am-5pm, Sept. - May

RCA STUDIO B — where country greats recorded their early hits. Artists like Elvis Presley, Dolly Parton, Jim Reeves. Corner of Music Square West and Roy Acuff Pl.; 242-9414. Hours: daily 9am-5pm

COUNTRY CROSSROADS — "Nashville's Musical Showplace," which is located on Music Row and includes a huge gift shop and five theatres that star computer-animated, 3-dimensional characters. 1510 Division St.; 242-7800. Hours: daily 8am-8pm, June - Aug.; daily 9am-5pm, Sept. - May

COUNTRY MUSIC HALL OF FAME — dedicated to entertainers, composers and leaders of the country music industry. 4 Music Square East; 244-2522. Hours: daily 8am-8pm, June - Aug.; daily 9am-5pm, Sept. - May

CUMBERLAND MUSEUM & SCIENCE CENTER — features laser light shows, live animals and major traveling exhibits. 800 Ridley Ave.; 259-6099. Hours: 9:30am-5pm, Tues - Sat.; 12:30pm-5pm, Sun.

THE HERMITAGE — the restored home of Andrew Jackson. 4580 Rachel's Lane; 889-2941. Hours: daily 9am-5pm

TULIP GROVE — restored home of Andrew Jackson Donelson. 4580 Rachel's Lane; 889-2941. Hours: daily 9am-5pm

CHEEKWOOD BOTANICAL GARDENS AND FINE ARTS CENTER — Art exhibitions are seen in this 60-room southern mansion, which is surrounded by gardens considered to be one of the finest in America. Forrest Park Dr.; 352-5310. Hours: 9am-5pm, Tues. - Sat.; 1pm-5pm, Sun.

THE BELLE MEADE MANSION — considered the "Queen" of Tennessee antebellum estates, it was built in 1853. Harding Rd. & Leake Ave.; 352-7350. Hours: 9am-5pm, Mon. - Sat.; 1pm-5pm, Sun.

THE UPPER ROOM — The world-famous wood carving of Leonardo da Vinci's "The Last Supper," and stained glass windows depicting Christian history are found in this chapel/museum. 1908 Grand Ave.; 327-2700. Hours: daily 8am-4:30pm

MUSIC ROW ENTERTAINMENT CENTER — a mall in the Music Row area which includes museums, attractions and shops. 115 16th Ave. South; 255-3411. Hours: Sun. - Thurs., 9am-5pm, Sept. - June 1, and Fri. - Sat., 9am-6pm; daily 9am-8pm, June 2 - Sept. 1

BELMONT MANSION — This 1850 mansion was the center of Nashville's social life for nearly half a century. Belmont Blvd.; 269-9537. Hours: 10am-4pm, Tues. - Sat.

TWITTY CITY — Home of country music star Conway Twitty, which has grown to become a huge tourist complex. 1 Music Village Blvd., Hendersonville, TN; 822-6650. Hours: 9am-10pm, May 1 - Labor Day; daily 9am-5pm, Sept. - April

MUSIC VILLAGE U.S.A. — adjacent to Twitty City, consists of country music shows and other attractions. Music Village Blvd., Hendersonville, TN; 824-4700. Hours: 8pm, Thurs. - Sat.

HOUSE OF CASH — This Johnny Cash museum contains many personal items of Johnny Cash and his wife, June Carter. One section of the museum is devoted to the Carter Family. 700 Johnny Cash Parkway, Hendersonville, TN; 824-5110. Hours: Mon. - Sat. 9am-5:30pm, June 1 - Sept.; Mon. - Sat. 9am-4:30pm, Oct. 1 - May 31

MAP B — NASHVILLE AREA

1. Jim Reeves Museum
2. Music Valley Wax Museum
3. Opryland
4. Grand Ole Opry
5. Tennessee State Museum
6. Tennessee Performing Arts Center
7. Fort Nashborough
8. Ryman Auditorium
9. Parthenon
10. Car Collector's Hall of Fame
11. RCA Studio B
12. Country Crossroads
13. Country Music Hall of Fame
14. Cumberland Museum & Science Center
15. The Hermitage
16. Tulip Grove
17. Cheekwood Botanical Gardens and Fine Arts Center
18. The Belle Meade Mansion
19. The Upper Room
20. Music Row Entertainment Center
21. Belmont Mansion
22. Twitty City
23. Music Village U.S.A.
24. House of Cash

QUOTATIONS

"It's the songs, songs with honesty such as 'AMANDA,' that made Nashville 'Music City.'"
— *Waylon Jennings (Songwriter/Recording Artist)*

"Willie Nelson was a young, new songwriter when he sang me 'HELLO WALLS' in a little beer joint called Tootsie's Orchid Lounge in Nashville. This song has been recorded over 300 times and has sold over 5 million records. You never know where or when you'll find a hit song."
— *Faron Young (Recording Artist)*

"The music industry is an essential factor to the Nashville economy and to Nashville's vitality."
— *Mayor Richard Fulton (Mayor of Nashville, Tennessee)*

"I've made one major mistake in my music/business career — not moving permanently to Nashville much sooner. It's great to be a part of the music community here in residence."
— *Charles Fach (President of Compleat Entertainment)*

"There are recording centers all over the world. Sometimes they're hot, sometimes they're cold. But Music City U.S.A. just keeps on rolling, because that's where most of the good songs are most of the time!"
— *Dickey Lee (Songwriter/Recording Artist)*

"There's more talent here on one square foot than any other place in the world."
— *Pete Drake (Producer/Publisher)*

"Nashville is unique in that it is the songwriting capital of the world. There are more great writers concentrated in the Music City area than any other place. Nashville has become the 'Mayo Clinic' of the music industry. Many artists suffering from the lack of a hit have turned to Nashville for the cure . . . that cure being the Nashville Song."
— *Frances W. Preston (Vice-President – BMI)*

"Los Angeles has always been known for its fine recording studios. New York has been known as the heart of the business aspect of the music industry. But Nashville has always been known for its songs and its musicians, which should only be taken as the greatest type of compliment. Over the years, Nashville has attracted every facet of music from Rhythm and Blues, Gospel, Rock-n-Roll and, of course, the greatest — Country Music."
— *Tony Brown (RCA Records – Nashville)*

"The Grand Ole Opry since 1925 has been the big attraction that has drawn singers, musicians, songwriters, publishers and recording studios from all over the world. In my case I drove up from Florida in a 1949 Mercury in June of 1956."
— *Mel Tillis (Songwriter/Recording Artist)*

"I love Nashville and being a part of its great music industry. Many of the songs listed in this book influenced my early musical training in the Smoky Mountains, fueling my dream of someday playing a major role in the network of singers, writers and publishers that makes Nashville the music capital of the world."
— *Ronnie Milsap (Recording Artist)*

"Great City. . . . Rewarding Business."
— *Dennis W. Morgan (Songwriter)*

"Nashville has become the Third Coast with its abundance of diversified talent and facilities. The entertainment industry, which includes all forms of music, film, video, commercials and jingles, is presently the third largest industry in the state of Tennessee. Nashville is truly the Tin Pan Alley of our time."
— *Dale Franklin Cornelius (Executive Director of Nashville Music Association)*

"Los Angeles is a musician's town, New York is a lawyer's town, Nashville is a songwriter's town. Songwriters have made Nashville 'Music City U.S.A.'"
— *Bob McDill (Songwriter)*

"Having lived in Nashville, working in the music industry since the 1950's, I have been in the fortunate position to watch Nashville and the music industry grow together. It's hard to imagine Nashville without a music industry, and even harder to imagine Music City U.S.A. being located anywhere but Nashville, Tennessee. The industry is a proud part of our community. The songs that made Nashville 'Music City U.S.A.' have made the world 'Music City U.S.A.'-conscious."
— *Buddy Killen (President and Chief Executive Officer of Tree International)*

"Nashville has become 'Music City U.S.A.' because its music is . . . from the heart."
— *David Houston (Songwriter)*

"Hillbilly Klondike: Singers, writers, players, promoters, hangers-on, and even a few pickpockets — all looking for the Mother Lode. Felice and I were blest in finding a very rich vein. Very exciting then — still is."
— *Boudleaux Bryant (Songwriter)*

"Country songs, most of which are created by Nashville writers, have lyrics of substance which relate to the realities of everyday life, thus giving them a memorable quality. This has made them one of the primary reasons why Nashville is known the world over as 'Music City U.S.A.'"

— *Joe Talbot (Joe Talbot & Associates, Inc. –Nashville)*

"Great Town — Great Music Town!"

— *Bob Beckham (President of Combine Music)*

"Nashville is the last bastion of creative songwriting and publishing in the world. It's the songs that keep Nashville on the map."

— *Bob Montgomery (Publisher)*

"I am currently doing all my recording in Nashville. I get a great feeling working with the Nashville pickers. There's a real freedom working with other creative people who understand my music. I think the Nashville group of musicians really let that creative freedom happen."

— *B.J. Thomas (Recording Artist)*

"As others, I found myself attracted to Nashville, a city which has provided me with an excellent opportunity and environment to pursue my chosen field in personal artist management."

— *Jackson Brumley (Manager for David Frizzell & Shelly West)*

"I think one of the main reasons Music City is famous is because it is the home of the Grand Ole Opry. The early recordings done by Paul Cohen, Steve Sholes and Owen Bradley became known as the Nashville Sound. I also feel the spirit of the music industry in Nashville in contrast to other markets is more friendly and downhome."

— *Connie Bradley (Southern Regional Executive Director –ASCAP)*

"The publishing of this book, in my opinion, is one of the most visionary efforts ever accomplished. To quote the phrase 'It all begins with a song' might seem trite; however, the songs within this book represent the very bedrock foundation of Nashville — 'Music City U.S.A.' It especially pleases me that songs of Good News called gospel have helped to lay stone upon stone of that solid foundation and continues to be a part of its exciting future."

— *Don Butler (Executive Director of The Gospel Music Association)*

"Music . . . it started back, long ago. Before the age of sound, Mother Nature lived alone. Then God gave her a child. Through a little girl named Music, God's Blessing could be heard. All at once, The Spirit of Music was felt throughout the world . . ."

— *Stan Webb (Songwriter)*

Special Edition With Full Music Arrangements Also Available!

The Songs That Made Nashville Music City U.S.A. is also available in an edition arranged for piano, voice and guitar. All 100 songs from the pocket book are included in arrangements that provide melody line, lyrics, piano accompaniment and guitar chord frames. Standard 9″ x 12″ music book size. **$12.95**

ORDER FORM

Please send me _____ copy(ies) of *The Songs That Made Nashville Music City U.S.A.* arranged for piano/vocal/guitar @ $12.95 each + $1.50 postage/handling.

Name:_____

Address:_____

City/State/Zip: _____

☐ Check/Money Order Enclosed   Acct. No._____

☐ MasterCard   Exp. Date_____

☐ VISA

☐ American Express   _____
                              CUSTOMER SIGNATURE

Mail to: Hal Leonard Publishing Corp., Dept. N
           8112 W. Bluemound Rd.
           P.O. Box 13819
           Milwaukee, WI 53213

Please allow 2-3 weeks for delivery.